The Dream of the Marsh Wren

THE *CREDO* SERIES

A *credo* is a statement of belief, an assertion of deep conviction. The *Credo* series offers contemporary American writers whose work emphasizes the natural world and the human community the opportunity to discuss their essential goals, concerns, and practices. Each volume presents an individual writer's *credo,* his or her investigation of what it means to write about human experience and society in the context of the more-than-human world, as well as a biographical profile and complete bibliography of the author's published work. The *Credo* series offers some of our best writers an opportunity to speak to the fluid and subtle issues of rapidly changing technology, social structure, and environmental conditions.

The Dream of the Marsh Wren

WRITING AS RECIPROCAL CREATION

Pattiann Rogers

Scott Slovic, *Credo* Series Editor

Credo

MILKWEED EDITIONS

Published 1999 by Milkweed Editions
Printed in the United States of America
Cover design by Rob Dewey
Cover painting by Fran Gregory
Author photo by H. Emerson Blake
Interior photo on p. 83 by Irene Tall
The text of this book is set in Stone Serif.
99 00 01 02 03   5 4 3 2 1
First Edition

Milkweed Editions is a not-for-profit publisher. We gratefully ac-
knowledge support from the Elmer L. and Eleanor J. Andersen
Foundation; James Ford Bell Foundation; Bush Foundation;
Dayton's, Mervyn's, and Target Stores by the Dayton Hudson
Foundation; Doherty, Rumble and Butler Foundation; General Mills
Foundation; Honeywell Foundation; Jerome Foundation; McKnight
Foundation; Minnesota State Arts Board through an appropriation
by the Minnesota State Legislature; Creation and Presentation
Programs of the National Endowment for the Arts; Norwest
Foundation on behalf of Norwest Bank Minnesota; Lawrence and
Elizabeth Ann O'Shaughnessy Charitable Income Trust in honor of
Lawrence M. O'Shaughnessy; Oswald Family Foundation; Piper
Jaffray Companies, Inc.; Ritz Foundation on behalf of Mr. and Mrs.
E. J. Phelps Jr.; John and Beverly Rollwagen Fund of the Minneapolis
Foundation; St. Paul Companies, Inc.; Star Tribune Foundation; Elly
Sturgis; Lila Wallace Reader's Digest Fund; and generous individuals.

Library of Congress Cataloging-in-Publication Data

Rogers, Pattiann, 1940–
    The dream of the Marsh Wren : writing as reciprocal creation /
Pattiann Rogers. — 1st ed.
        p.   cm. — (Credo)
    Includes bibliographical references.
    ISBN 1-57531-228-5 (cl). — ISBN 1-57531-225-0 (pbk.)
    I. Title. II. Series: Credo (Minneapolis, Minn.)
PS3563.0454D7   1999
811'.54—dc21   98-50946
                                                          CIP

This book is dedicated with abundant gratitude to my teachers at Irving Elementary School, South Junior High School, Joplin Senior High School, the University of Missouri-Columbia, and the University of Houston, and especially to John Neihardt, Cynthia Macdonald, and my teacher by correspondence from the University of Washington, Nelson Bentley.

The Dream of the Marsh Wren

The Dream of the Marsh Wren

The Dream of the Marsh Wren

WRITING AS RECIPROCAL CREATION

by Pattiann Rogers

The Dream of the Marsh Wren: Reciprocal Creation

The marsh wren, furtive and tail-tipped,
by the rapid brown blurs of his movements
makes sense of the complexities of sticks
and rushes. He makes slashes and complicated
lines of his own in mid-air above the marsh
by his flight and the rattles of his incessant
calling. He exists exactly as if he were a product
of the pond and the sky and the blades of light
among the reeds and grasses, as if he were
deliberately willed into being by the empty
spaces he eventually inhabits.

And at night, inside each three-second
shudder of his sporadic sleep, understand
how he creates the vision of the sun
blanched and barred by the diagonal juttings
of the weeds, and then the sun as heavy
cattail crossed and tangled and rooted
deep in the rocking of its own gold water,

3

and then the sun as suns in flat explosions
at the bases of the tule. Inside the blink
of his eyelids, understand how he composes
the tule dripping sun slowly in gold rain
off its black edges, and how he composes
gold circles widening on the blue surface
of the sun's pond, and the sharp black
slicing of his wing rising against the sun,
and that same black edge skimming the thin
corridor of gold between sky and pond.

Imagine the marsh wren making himself
inside his own dream. Imagine the wren,
created by the marsh, inside the marsh
of his own creation, unaware of his being
inside this dream of mine where I imagine
he dreams within the boundaries of his own
fixed black eye around which this particular
network of glistening weeds and knotted
grasses and slow-dripping gold mist
and seeded winds shifting in waves of sun
turns and tangles and turns itself completely
inside out again here composing me
in the stationary silence of its only existence.

I was thirty-one and living, for the second summer,
in a new suburb outside Houston, Texas. Until the
previous year, I had lived all of my life in small towns
in southwest Missouri. I had one very young son and
one baby son who were inexplicably and wonder-
fully napping at the same time.

I'd been outdoors gathering up their toys scat-
tered in the yard and had come into the house out

of a hurting summer heat of semitropical intensity that I hadn't yet become accustomed to, a truly palpable heat, a heat even the eyes could feel, a heavy, moist, fiery, unrelieved encumbrance that made merely thinking seem an act too energetic to perform.

The flat, grass-splotched yard of our new home, in a subdivision boasting houses with four different floor plans, contained one tree possessing a trunk two inches in diameter and eight spindly branches. I checked these branches each morning for signs of new leaves, the buds of new sprouts. If it's true that human attention and caressing can cause trees to produce profuse foliage, then our willow oak should have shot above the rooftop. In short, however, we had no shade.

I entered the dark, air-conditioned house on this July afternoon, the windows shut tight, the curtains drawn to ease the burden of cooling. I was covered with perspiration. My bare feet were still burning. I stood still for a moment until my eyes adjusted to the darkness, then walked into the bedroom and lay down across the bed.

I didn't like where I was living.

There was nothing wrong with the new house, which was the largest, most convenient I'd ever lived in. And my neighbors were friendly and engaged, as we were, in raising young children. But I felt alone here, abandoned, unnurtured, displaced, unknown. I wasn't in tears yet, but very close to it. I wanted to go back to Missouri. It was the first time I'd said it outright, understanding, in my situation, the impossible desperation of such an admission. But I knew it to be true.

As I lay there, the blessed air conditioner roaring and humming, I decided to close my eyes and try to remember what it was like in Missouri, in the Ozark hills and woods in the fall, my favorite season. I tried to recall every detail I could and to name each detail to myself, to recreate the land with language—the sharp angle of the gold autumn light, the thin feel of the air, the fragrances of trees and damp earth, auras of moving shadows in a dense forest, the abundances of bronze oak leaves and yellow hickory leaves and walnut, wine and scarlet hedges of staghorn sumac, the rocky earth, sometimes orange with iron, grey-green curls of lichen on boulders, frost and its graces on the ground, the sight of breath on cold air, the taste of October.

Creating this litany brought a strange, calm comfort to me, a joy I hadn't expected, and during those moments I realized for the first time that I loved a landscape, loved it like my own body, that it *was* my own body, my body and my pattern of perception, that it had informed and constructed me, that I had defined myself by it, that I had a union with it, a union I only recognized now because it had been broken. This naming of details of the land and season, this litany, recited to myself in a moment of despair, eventually became, during the next few days, my first poem coming from the earth, submerged in the earth. Although I'd been writing poems off and on for several years, mostly in fixed forms, this was a poem of a different kind.

But, possibly even more important, I realized in those moments a power of the language that I hadn't been fully aware of before, a power beyond relaying information or instruction, beyond rhetoric or making patterns, rhyme and meter, on a page. It was a power I could possess, the power of my own creation to enter and alter my soul. The language had created me. This thought of reciprocal creation has remained central to my writing since.

All of this happened ten years before my first published book. And for twenty years I lived in that same house. Our willow oak, our magnolia, our elm, spread and blossomed and eventually rose above our roof. During those years I learned how to find the affirmation and beauty of the Texas landscape around me, to identify and take sustenance from it, so new, so strange to me at first. And I learned that home is wherever the people I love live, the people for whom I am responsible, the people who depend on me as I depend on them. I believe the land anywhere, the earth, responds to and encourages and itself takes sustenance from such human bonds.

———————

I'm often asked why I write and, specifically, why I write poetry, and how a poem begins, the process involved in writing a poem. I give many different answers to these questions, all equally true, all equally invented, all equally partial, all equally erroneous, all realigning and altering themselves among themselves. I can only guess, as honestly as I can, as to why I write and how I write. The process of writing is too mysterious, at least too mysterious to me, to be accurately explained. Thank goodness. And to claim that I understand myself so well would be arrogant in the extreme.

However, I want to offer a few of the easier and simpler answers to the question of why I write poetry and then to try to delineate other complexities behind what I believe motivates me to write. First, I write poetry because it's something I discovered I could do. It isn't really true that we can be or do anything we want, although I'm not sorry my father told me this over and over as I was growing up. I could never play football on the defensive line of the Broncos, for instance. Scratch that possibility. I could never be a Hollywood sex goddess. Wrong body. I tried tap dancing, my father's wish, at Mary Ann Hatley's School of the Dance. That was a disaster. I tried the piano. My hands never ceased being stiff as claws and mechanical as wind-up toys. But I discovered I had a little talent for writing.

While an undergraduate at the University of Missouri, I took a course in verse writing taught by John Neihardt. We wrote two poems a week during that semester, all in assigned forms, sonnets, Spenserian stanzas, blank verse, among many others. The last assignment of the semester was to write a poem modeled on the form of "Sea Fever" by John Masefield. This is a poem of three rhyming quatrains with a rather difficult meter containing several spondees, two accented syllables coming together. I was the only person in the class able to write a poem in this form. It was then that I realized I could do something other people found difficult.

"The Dawn That Day" is the title of the poem. It was written in l961 and is included in a small chapbook I had printed four years later at my own expense. The meter isn't exactly like Masefield's in a couple of places, but I did get the spondees and the two-syllable rhymes where they appear in "Sea Fever."

The Dawn That Day

The dawn that day, coming gray-tinted, seemed earlier
    to me.
I watched to see on the cold hills how it lent serenity.
But I turned quick as a bed creaked and a door shut
    lightly,
And you loomed large by our small hearth where the
    fire blazed brightly.

I watched you dress in the half-light that played softly
    on your form
And felt your hand with its broad palm come to touch
    me, sure and warm.
The sun rose and the light spread and the hour crept
    nearer.
And the bright day made our thoughts real, and our
    task seemed clearer.

I heard their feet as you stood erect and heard you say
    goodbye.

The sky loomed large and the drums beat and I heard
    the children cry.
The dust blew and the feet marched and I watched you
    leaving,
While the wind cried and the sun wept and my world
    lay grieving.

It seemed important to me to work to develop any talent for writing I might possess, as if this talent were a gift given to me and it would be a discourtesy to ignore it, to refuse to accept it.

I learned something else significant in that class. John Neihardt was the first person I'd ever heard read poetry the way it should be read. He chanted. He intoned. He sang. Hearing him read, I understood that poetry is essentially, and above all, music.

And I write poetry because I like to write it and because I never get bored with writing it. Writing poetry is full of play, whimsy, experimentation with cadences, sounds, forms, definitions, structures, subtleties, suggestion. Occasionally, not always, that play gains momentum and depth and breaks into new dominions of thought and perception. Working within its craft and art, writing poetry possesses a freedom of thought I've never experienced in any other activity. And I love the English language and its music. I marvel at my huge dictionary I can hardly lift, at all my field guides filled with words and their definitions, detailing the features and life of the earth. I cherish my CD-ROM containing the entire Oxford English Dictionary. Someone told me recently that the English language contains ten thousand syllables, ten thousand different sounds, and that means infinite possibilities of combinations of sounds and rhythms. I like to explore those possibilities through poetry. I can take a sheet of blank paper or an empty computer screen and with a word or two open a door, a gate, into another realm, a world I can construct and simultaneously enter to explore as I wish, leading and being led by the music, pace, sound and form, the meanings and connotations of the words. I can create a new experience with language. So, purely on a selfish note, writing poetry is fun for me. It's exciting, and I want to do it over and over. I don't mean it isn't work. It is. And there are many, many failures and frustrations. But it's the kind of work that totally engages me, that challenges me in ways I like.

And then, sometimes I write poetry because I'm afraid, altogether solitary and uncertain in an uncertain world, and I want something still and close and clear and unchanging to be one with me. The right poem can be that. And that right poem can also be an offering, an offering I make, the very best offering I know how to make, in exchange for redemption, expiation, for acceptance, for rescue, for love.

These are not my only reasons for writing. But they may be the easiest to articulate.

———

I believe I can talk with a measure of confidence about how any particular poem happened to begin and the place of its origin. But I can't talk about the process involved in actually writing the poem. I don't know what is happening then. It's too complicated. It involves learning and practicing all the crafts and arts inherent to writing poetry. It means allowing longings and despairs, wishes and bewilderments, terrors, serenities, joys and loves, all to enter the writing and have their voices. But the writing also involves a feeling of the way, as if in a kind of blindness, moving along in total darkness, feeling the way forward with the body, with all the faculties, feeling the way with the language, hoping not to run into a rock wall or to step off into a bottomless chasm, the call trailing off, disappearing and lost.

Coincident with our move to Texas from Missouri, and the revelations about land and language that accompanied that change in my life, were the births of my two sons. I wanted very early, before I had any serious thoughts of being a writer, to be the best mother I could be. That was my first and primary goal. During their infant and young childhood years, I gave almost all my time, energy, and thought to that work. I still consider being a mother the most important and significant work of my life. What I may have lost in writing time during the years when my children were growing up was more than amply compensated for by all they gave to me, all that they continue to give. For me, writing was never more important than these human beings who were dependent on me in vital ways.

Many of my poems were influenced by my

children, by my participation in their first discovery and meeting with the world, by their curiosity and energy and undoubting faith in the goodness of life and their closeness to the earth, by my love for them and my identification with them. They allowed me to see life with their eyes, and I saw life anew. "Intermediary" is a poem written specifically for them.

Intermediary
for John A. and Arthur

This is what I ask: that if they must be taken
They be taken like the threads of the cotton grass
Are taken by the summer wind, excited and dizzy
And safe, flying inside their own seeds;
And if they must be lost that they be lost
Like leaves of the water starwort
Are lost, submerged and rising over and over
In the slow-rooted current by the bank.

I ask that they always be found
With the same sure and easy touch
The early morning stillness uses to find itself
In needles of dew on each hyssop in the ditch.

And may they see everything the boatman bug,
Shining inside its bubble of air, sees
Through silver skin in the pond-bottom mud,
And may they be obliged in the same way the orb snail,
Sucking on sedges in shallow water, is obliged.
And may they be promised everything a single blade
Of sweet flag, kept by the grip of the elmid
On its stem, kept by the surrounding call

Of the cinnamon teal, kept by its line
In the marsh-filled sky, is promised.

Outloud, in public and in writing, I ask again
That solace come to them like sun comes
To the egg of the longspur, penetrating the shell,
Settling warmth inside the potential heart
And beginnings of bone. And I ask that they remember
Their grace in the same way the fetal bird remembers
    light
Inside the blackness of its gathering skull inside
The cave of its egg.

And with the same attention a streamer of ice
Moving with the moon commands, with the same
    decision
The grassland plovers declare as they rise
From the hayfields into the evening sky,
I ask that these pleas of mine arrest the notice
Of all those angels already possessing a lasting love
For fine and dauntless boys like mine.

Although few of my poems directly address ex-
periences with my children, they are everywhere
throughout my work. The following incident, for ex-
ample, led to the writing of a poem contained in my
first book.

One spring evening when my son Arthur was
around seven years old, I noticed that the neighbor-
hood children were gathering in our garage. Some-
thing told me I should probably go out and see what
this was about. When I arrived, I saw Arthur up in
the rafters of the garage, jumping from two-by-four

to two-by-four, attempting to catch a baby bird that had flown in and become confused.

Alarmed at the sight of this dangerous activity, I said, in my calmest voice, "Artie, why don't you come down now and let the mother and father bird take care of the baby?"

But Arthur had this adoring audience watching below, and, stumbling, nearly missing the next two-by-four, he shouted down to me, "This is what I love to do—help Mother Nature."

My memory of the next few moments is a complete blank, but somehow Arthur caught the bird and got safely down, amid much excitement. Finally a real, living bird in the hand after many failed attempts in the past to secure one. Arthur is the child who tried to lure a bird into his clutches by dropping a trail of bread pieces up the sidewalk to our front door where he intended to hide until some gullible bird came within reach. One problem with this plan was that our dog, Loki, discovered the bread trail first and gobbled up all the bread before Arthur even got settled behind the door to wait.

Arthur wanted, of course, to keep this baby bird. It was almost dark and we had a cat and I didn't see any concerned adult birds hovering nearby. So I agreed that we would keep the bird overnight, on the condition that we let it go in the morning so that it could be cared for properly by its parents. We put it in an old bird cage and settled it inside Arthur's closet, where it continued to cheep and chirp periodically throughout the night.

The next morning, in the haste and confusion of preparing the children for school—Arthur, who never wanted to go to school—lagging along as usual, there was no time to release the baby bird with the ceremony such an event deserved. After the children were gone, I had what I thought was a good idea. I would put the bird cage with the baby bird in it out under our crape myrtle bushes, and then if the parents were around, they would hear it and come. I did this, and before I got back to the house, a father cardinal had flown to the cage. I hadn't realized that the baby bird was a cardinal. There was much happy reunion and greeting between father and baby, calling and cheeping. At the same time I saw the father cardinal, so did our cat, seeming to be both delighted and intrigued with this bird commotion. When the father cardinal saw the cat, he began to feign injury, hoping to distract the cat from his fledgling, flopping in a pretended struggle to rise, one wing held straight out. The cat was crouched low now on the lawn, ready to spring, totally focused on this beautiful red bird staying so wonderfully within cat-reach.

"My God, this is going to be a tragedy," I thought and went running as fast as I could and fell on the cat, who felt like solid steel. All the lax bonelessness of his usual state had completely disappeared. I grabbed him up quickly and held tight. I knew if I put him in the house he would find some way of getting out before I could take care of the bird. So I put him in the car. I can still see the expression on his face as he watched out the car window, "What in the world is going on here?"—the delicious father cardinal continuing to flop on the ground.

I had to decide what to do next. This bird, this baby cardinal, was Arthur's bird. I knew when he came home from school, if the bird were gone, the cage empty, there would be trouble. So I got in the car with the cat and we drove to the school to get Arthur. I explained the situation to his teacher, and Arthur, who was overjoyed to be released from school-prison, and I and the cat headed home. I told Arthur about the father cardinal, and he agreed that we must let the bird go right away.

We had a small ceremony in the backyard, the bird held in both of Arthur's hands. Then he opened his hands and released the bird, who went flying away, wobbly, up into our elm, where it was immediately attacked by a blue jay. "Is this saga never going to end?" I thought. But the father cardinal was there right away and charged the blue jay, driving it off. All seemed to be concluding satisfactorily, except that Arthur didn't want to return to school.

Later in the day, thinking on these events, I wondered, "What would life look like to you if everything good you knew in the world came from a redbird? What, if when you called in fear or longing, it was a redbird who answered, when you were hungry, it was a redbird who brought food, when you were threatened, it was a redbird who drove danger away? How would you interpret your life? How would you perceive and define your experiences?"

This event with Arthur and the questions that

followed were the beginning of the poem, "Suppose Your Father Was a Redbird," a poem of supposition, the exploration of a supposition, a type of poem I like to write.

Suppose Your Father Was a Redbird

Suppose his body was the meticulous layering
Of graduated down which you studied early,
Rows of feathers increasing in size to the hard-splayed
Wine-gloss tips of his outer edges.

Suppose, before you could speak, you watched
The slow spread of his wing over and over,
The appearance of that invisible appendage,
The unfolding transformation of his body to the
	airborne.
And you followed his departure again and again,
Learning to distinguish the red microbe of his being
Far into the line of the horizon.

Then today you might be the only one able to see
The breast of a single red bloom
Five miles away across an open field.
The modification of your eye might have enabled you
To spot a red moth hanging on an oak branch
In the exact center of the Aurorean Forest.
And you could define for us "hearing red in the air,"
As you predict the day pollen from the poppy
Will blow in from the valley.

Naturally you would picture your faith arranged
In filamented principles moving from pink
To crimson at the final quill. And the red tremble

Of your dream you might explain as the shimmer
Of his back lost over the sea at dawn.
Your sudden visions you might interpret as the
    uncreasing
Of heaven, the bones of the sky spread,
The conceptualized wing of the mind untangling.

Imagine the intensity of your revelation
The night the entire body of a star turns red
And you watch it as it rushes in flames
Across the black, down into the hills.

If your father was a redbird,
Then you would be obligated to try to understand
What it is you recognize in the sun
As you study it again this evening
Pulling itself and the sky in dark red
Over the edge of the earth.

I've often felt that many of our abstractions are
structured or embedded in something concrete, that
we come partially to understand our abstractions by
understanding the concrete objects to which they are
attached and so defined. This isn't a new thought. It's
what metaphor is all about. As a very young child, I
pictured the word "day" as a half circle of white
wood, "noon" as a full vision of black/yellow light,
and I still picture the seasons, as they pertain to time,
on a wheel laid horizontally before me, heart-high,
winter closest to me, summer on the farther side. I
envision where I am on that wheel.

Whatever else this Texas land happened to be, it
was clearly abundant with life—insects everywhere,

crickets, cicadas, fire ants, roaches, some three inches long, and birds, cattle egrets, grackles, martins, song birds, reptiles of all kinds, anoles, snakes. There were frogs and slider turtles, pancake turtles in the bayou-type ditches of the fields surrounding our subdivision. I once drove my son John home in our small Volkswagen after one of his jaunts into this wilderness. It was his habit to send his brother or one of his friends to fetch me if he'd found something too large to carry home. His catch this time, a snapping turtle the size of a dinner plate, kept climbing out of a bucket at my feet on the floor of the car. And I was wearing sandals. This is the only time I ever remember deliberately running a stop sign. We generally kept the animals he caught for a few days, watching and touching them, and then we returned them to where they were found.

Crawdads after any heavy rain were washed out of their burrows in the fields and into the gutters of our street in great numbers. A population explosion of toads occurred one year. They were so numerous beneath the streetlights at night that it was difficult to walk through the moving morass of them without stepping on one. Reach down and bring up a handful of mud anywhere in our neighborhood, and it was certain to contain life of some sort.

I used to accompany my son John on his forays into the flat fields and drainage ditches surrounding our house during the years when he was three, four, five years old, too young to go alone. I didn't go with him to instruct or guide him, heaven forbid, but to keep him from getting lost or in a dangerous situation, to stay out of his way and allow him to explore as he wished. The thought about abstractions and their concrete objects occurred to me one day as I was sitting in the field watching him. I wondered how he was structuring his world, into what forms he might be embodying his definitions of abstractions.

Concepts and Their Bodies
(The Boy in the Field Alone)

Staring at the mud turtle's eye
Long enough, he sees *concentricity* there
For the first time, as if it possessed
Pupil and iris and oracular lid,
As if it grew, forcing its own gene of circularity.
The concept is definitely
The cellular arrangement of sight.

The five amber grasses maintaining their seedheads
In the breeze against the sky
Have borne *latitude* from the beginning,
Secure *civility* like leaves in their folds.
He discovers *persistence* in the mouth
Of the caterpillar in the same way
As he discovers clear syrup
On the broken end of the dayflower,
Exactly as he comes accidently upon
The mud crown of the crawfish.

The spotted length of the bullfrog leaping
Lakeward just before the footstep
Is not bullfrog, spread and sailing,

But the body of *initiative* with white glossy belly.
Departure is the wing let loose
By the dandelion, and it does possess
A sparse down and will not be thought of,
Even years later, even in the station
At midnight among the confusing lights,
As separate from that white twist
Of filament drifting.

Nothing is sharp enough to disengage
The butterfly's path from *erraticism.*

And *freedom* is this September field
Covered this far by tree shadows
Through which this child chooses to run
Until he chooses to stop,
And it will be so hereafter.

Many of my poems, as I understand them, rise
not from one motivation, but from many, not from a
single aim but multiple intentions and beliefs shift-
ing and modifying, overlapping and affecting one
another. And the poems make themselves as they
come into being, occasioning unanticipated images,
questions, and directions, creating belief in their mo-
ments. The poem "Rolling Naked in the Morning
Dew" originated from several separate experiences—
watching my two sons rolling down a grassy hill in
Missouri one spring morning, participating vicari-
ously in their unrestrained exhilaration, and remem-
bering similar childhood experiences of my own,
rolling over and over and how earth and sky changed
places again and again during that spinning, how

much affirmation and joy that simple activity engendered, and recalling other times when I was literally face-to-face with the earth, lying beneath big piles of dry oak leaves next to damp ground, the acrid scent, the dry crackling, the tingling anticipation before bursting forth into the sunlight, or making a secret hideout deep inside the thick tent-shadows of a trumpet vine in blossom. Then I read of Lillie Langtry rolling naked in the dew. All of these elements, coming together with my love of words of naming, became the starting point of this poem.

Rolling Naked in the Morning Dew

Out among the wet grasses and wild barley-covered
Meadows, backside, frontside, through the white clover
And feather peabush, over spongy tussocks
And shaggy-mane mushrooms, the abandoned nests
Of larks and bobolinks, face to face
With vole trails, snail niches, jelly
Slug eggs; or in a stone-walled garden, level
With the stemmed bulbs of orange and scarlet tulips,
Cricket carcasses, the bent blossoms of sweet william,
Shoulder over shoulder, leg over leg, clear
To the ferny edge of the goldfish pond—some people
Believe in the rejuvenating powers of this act—naked
As a toad in the forest, belly and hips, thighs
And ankles drenched in the dew-filled gulches
Of oak leaves, in the soft fall beneath yellow birches,
All of the skin exposed directly to the *killy* cry
Of the king bird, the buzzing of grasshopper sparrows,
Those calls merging with the dawn-red mists

Of crimson steeplebush, entering the bare body then
Not merely through the ears but through the skin
Of every naked person willing every event and
    potentiality
Of a damp transforming dawn to enter.

Lillie Langtry practiced it, when weather permitted,
Lying down naked every morning in the dew,
With all of her beauty believing the single petal
Of her white skin could absorb and assume
That radiating purity of liquid and light.
And I admit to believing myself, without question,
In the magical powers of dew on the cheeks
And breasts of Lillie Langtry believing devotedly
In the magical powers of early morning dew on the
    skin
Of her body lolling in purple beds of bird's-foot violets,
Pink prairie mimosa. And I believe, without doubt,
In the mystery of the healing energy coming
From that wholehearted belief in the beneficent results
Of the good delights of the naked body rolling
And rolling through all the silked and sun-filled,
Dusky-winged, sheathed and sparkled, looped
And dizzied effluences of each dawn
Of the rolling earth.

Just consider how the mere idea of it alone
Has already caused me to sing and sing
This whole morning long.

I believe that any good and valid poem is an ex-
perience of its own, an experience of words and
sounds that shake the body and stun the senses, a
real experience in the real world. I believe a poem is

this first, no matter how else someone may define or interpret it intellectually. It has being, a time and a space of its own. It is not simply *about* a human experience, it *is* a human experience.

Naming is a distinctly human activity and one that can bestow honor. Sometimes I used to think, "Poor stars, the ones that have no name, missing that element of reality." Some of my poems have been motivated by my desire to honor a particular creature or plant or aspect of the natural world with words, my way of acknowledging my respect and appreciation for the beauty or courage, the faith or fearlessness, the devotion to life, the tenacity inherent to the living, nonhuman world, to capture and keep a moment by constructing its portrait in words. In such poems I want to depict as accurately as I can, in as much detail as I can and in the most evocative language possible, the integrity of whatever very specific entity it is I'm addressing. I think of these poems as being poems of praise or celebration. Sometimes poems that begin in this way go beyond their specific subjects, by means of their specific subjects, to address wider topics, but not always.

After our move to the Texas Gulf Coast, I had a close look at hermit crabs for the first time, and I was touched by the endurance and adaptation embodied in this vulnerable creature, moving along in its world, making its way, in its way, in the vast. But that vague feeling was not actual until the writing of the poem brought it into its full reality, informing me. This is the way I like my poems to function. I like to begin writing with a feeling imperfectly expressed and only partially understood and then advance with the writing, if possible, to a new level of clarity that brings awareness and appreciation to me. Perhaps the rhythm of the surf helped the motion of this poem.

Eulogy for a Hermit Crab

You were consistently brave
On these surf-drenched rocks, in and out of their salty
Slough holes around which the entire expanse
Of the glinting grey sea and the single spotlight
Of the sun went spinning and spinning and spinning
In a tangle of blinding spume and spray
And pistol-shot collisions your whole life long.
You stayed. Even with the wet icy wind of the moon
Circling your silver case night after night after night
You were here.

And by the gritty orange curve of your claws,
By the soft, wormlike grip
Of your hinter body, by the unrelieved wonder
Of your black-pea eyes, by the mystified swing
And swing and swing of your touching antennae,
You maintained your name meticulously, you kept
Your name intact exactly, day after day after day.
No one could say you were less than perfect
In the hermitage of your crabness.

Now, beside the racing, incomprehensible racket
Of the sea stretching its great girth forever
Back and forth between this direction and another,

Please let the words of this proper praise I speak
Become the identical and proper sound
Of my mourning.

My son John caught a horned lizard once when we were hiking in dry lands in California. I thought it was rather an unremarkable, ugly little thing, although I quite admired it, out there all on its own, surviving with an unquestioning and tenacious hold on life. A short time later, a photograph of a horned lizard appeared on the cover of an issue of *Ranger Rick*, a magazine I subscribed to for my children and generally read and enjoyed myself. I happened to be put off at this same time by the whining and complaining I was encountering from so many of my human contemporaries, as if they felt life weren't worth the effort, their lives so relatively comfortable and safe. The comparison was obvious. And thus began the poem.

Justification of the Horned Lizard

I don't know why the horned lizard wants to live.
It's so ugly—short prickly horns and scowling
Eyes, lipless smile forced forever by bone,
Hideous scaly hollow where its nose should be.

I don't know what the horned lizard has to live for,
Skittering over the sun-irritated sand, scraping
The hot dusty brambles. It never sees anything but
    gravel
And grit, thorns and stickery insects, the towering
Creosote bush, the ocotillo and its whiplike

Branches, the severe edges of the Spanish dagger.
Even shade is either barren rock or barb.

The horned lizard will never know
A lush thing in its life. It will never see the flower
Of the water-filled lobelia bent over a clear
Shallow creek. It will never know moss floating
In waves in the current by the bank or the blue-blown
Fronds of the water clover. It will never have a smooth
Glistening belly of white like the bullfrog or a dew-
     heavy
Trill like the mating toad. It will never slip easily
Through mud like the skink or squat in the dank
     humus
At the bottom of a decaying forest in daytime.
It will never be free of dust. The only drink it will ever
     know
Is in the body of a bug.

And the horned lizard possesses nothing noble—
Embarrassing tail, warty hide covered with sharp dirty
Scales. No touch to its body, even from its own kind,
Could ever be delicate or caressing.

I don't know why the horned lizard wants to live.
Yet threatened, it burrows frantically into the sand
With a surprisingly determined fury of forehead, limbs
And ribs. Pursued, it even fights for itself, almost rising
     up,
Posturing on its bowed legs, propelling blood out of its
     eyes
In tight straight streams shot directly at the source
Of its possible extinction. It fights for itself,
Almost rising up, as if the performance of that act,

The posture, the propulsion of the blood itself,
Were justification enough and the only reason needed.

Another poem that I view as beginning from my wish to discover a particular creature more completely and to honor it, is "Fetal Bat: The Creation of the Void." There are many caves in northwest Arkansas, and when I was teaching at the University of Arkansas one winter, I went spelunking with some of my students. On the ceiling of the cave we entered were many small bats in hibernation, looking like brown, furry golf balls hanging from the rock walls. We were cautioned not to touch them, because they would wake, expend energy, and possibly not have sufficient energy then to make it through their winter hibernation. This event, happening in conjunction with my coming across a photograph of a fetal bat preserved in a jar, caused me to think again about bats, their being warm-blooded, their having live births, female bats nursing their infants, bat milk. I'd never truly imagined such a thing before. It seemed amazing, somehow, a pregnant bat hanging upside down in a cave, an infant bat being born. Sex, conception, the beginning of life, the moment when that boundary between the inert and the living is crossed and all the ramifications inherent to that moment—these subjects are a wonder to me, such common, everyday occurrences, and yet so absolutely astonishing every time they happen. The following poem, necessitating a little research, began as a result of all of these interests and events. It moves into a metaphysical thought at the end that hadn't occurred to me until I was working on the poem.

Fetal Bat: The Creation of the Void

Tender in its absolute predestination—four
long, deformed finger bones, plum-round
body, umbrella wings—it's an inevitability
begun by bat penis, sperm dart, bat
ovum, bat pocket of womb where it flutters,
flickers sporadically, warm and drowned
in swaying pearl-clear waters.

The fetus folds in its place, tightens,
settles again, shoulder-hunched knuckles
drawn to its ears, a vestigial claw
to its chin. Its eyes are thinly lidded.
Its tongue, slender, pliable as a single
leaflet of summer fern, moves back
slightly in its throat as if to suckle.

A pea-sized heart swings inside
the tiny night of its chest inside the night
behind its mother's nipples and blue
coming-milk inside the still stone cavern
of night where she hangs by one foot upside
down inside the universe of night
with its shifting, combusting summary
of stars wheeling inside, outside.

When this fetus of the wonderment emerges,
feet first, born alive, clinging
to its mother's teat, legs curled

beneath her arm pit, drying the fine fuzz
of its face and features, the translucent
dun and veined-scarlet silk skin
of its wings stretched wide, it screams,
screeches wildly, setting every petal
of yucca and sweet chicory that blooms
inside its rare garden to shivering,
to ringing.

O what a very first phenomenon
it makes as it occupies so perfectly
such a definite empty space, the only void
of itself which we recognize now
never anywhere, until this moment
of its birth, existed at all.

Often the subject of a poem is not only what it appears ostensibly to be. By addressing directly a specific subject or object, the poem can also address something else, something that might be difficult to address otherwise because of the limitations and clumsiness of our language. This is a form of metaphor, and in my opinion it is the strongest tool available to a poet.

I believe each nonhuman life is an expression somehow of an aspect of myself, if I were only clever enough to decipher all of those messages. I am comforted, pleased by the belief that the brook trout is the sleek-scaled and graceful aspect of myself that knows how to survive under water, the octopus the means by which I can discover the sea-world in a supple eight-ways simultaneously, the cushion cactus the part of myself that ingeniously flourishes with lavender-red flowers in the austerity of the desert, the wide maple the way I might seek in all directions at once, the brown bear my power to rise and tower, setting forests to quivering. The bat and the coyote allow me to touch the moon in gestures I could never achieve alone. By the undulating sky-circle of the hawk, I share in a sailing talent.

I have assumed this variety of life would always be present around me, life living at the same time as I am living, assumed that what happens to any of us will always happen within the context of this great march and pattern and carnival of nonhuman lives and that what we are is both illuminated and enriched by this context. What would happen if one day I walked out the door and it were all gone—no grasses seeding on their own, responding to wind or rain or sun or fire, responding with me to weather, no tree-pattern of life against the sky, vulnerable, as I am, to sudden tragedy, no purposeful hum of insect wings, no quick finch-flutter, flight and protest, no sun-flick of spine and fin in still water, no tiny motion of light midair indicating intention—all so blessedly, so blessedly, absorbed in their own affairs, the crucial business of maintaining life? What if this community, this community of my life, were gone, not only as species or as individuals, but vanished as aspects of myself, and gone as vivid proof, a tangible statement about life? That would be a loneliness like no other loneliness. Then it would truly be so—we would be alone in the universe.

Before I Wake

The turning of the marsh marigold coming slowly
Into its emergent bloom underwater; the turning
Of the coral sands over themselves and over their dunes
And over the scratchings of the scarab beetles
Turning over the dung of the desert doe; the pivoting
Of the eye of the bluefish turning inside the drawing
    light
Of its multiple school shifting its constellation
In the dark sea; this is the prayer of sleep
In which I lay myself down to dream.

The quiet enclosed by the burrowing wolf spider
Dragging its egg sac to the surface to sun;
The stillness covered by the barren strawberry
Making its fleshless seed on the rocky hill;
The study in the desert mushroom knotting itself
In the arid heat; the silence of the fetal sea horses
Bound in the pouch of their father; this is the dream
Of the soul in which I lay myself down to pray.

And I've asked the outward motion of the hollow web
Of the elm making leaf, and I've asked the inward
    motion
Of every glinting fin making the focus of the carp,
And I've asked the involution of the egg buds carried
In the dark inside the cowbirds circling overhead,
And I've asked the tight coiling and breaking
Of light traveling in the beads of the sawgrass
And the net of the sea oats splitting and binding
And splitting again over and over across the open lands
To keep me in this dream tonight through one prayer
    more.

———————

Writers who incorporate imagery from the non-human world in their work, who suggest that they are sustained by those images, are often accused of not adequately acknowledging the pitiless cruelty and violence present in nature and of ignoring the repulsive, annoying, dangerous aspects of wilderness. I began the writing of the following two poems specifically to address these issues and to acknowledge to myself and declare for myself these aspects of life on earth. Whatever else these poems may be, they were begun with this intention.

Geocentric

Indecent, self-soiled, bilious
reek of turnip and toadstool
decay, dribbling the black oil
of wilted succulents, the brown
fester of rotting orchids,
in plain view, that stain
of stinkhorn down your front,
that leaking roil of bracket
fungi down your back, you
purple-haired, grainy-fuzzed
smolder of refuse, fathering
fumes and boils and powdery
mildews, enduring the constant
interruption of sink-mire
flatulence, contagious
with ear wax, corn smut,
blister rust, backwash
and graveyard debris, rich

with manure bog and dry-rot
harboring not only egg-addled
garbage and wrinkled lip
of orange-peel mold but also
the clotted breath of overripe
radish and burnt leek, bearing
every dank, malodorous rut
and scarp, all sulphur fissures
and fetid hillside seepages, old,
old, dependable, engendering
forever the stench and stretch
and warm seeth of inevitable
putrefaction, nobody
loves you as I do.

Roger Weingarten calls "Geocentric" "a love poem
to the planet." He writes in *Poetry East,* "I used to
think that the romantic poet was one who believed
that roses grew in garbage heaps; I accepted Isaac
Babel's view of the romantic as the near-sighted sol-
dier who preferred to see the world without his spec-
tacles. After reading 'Geocentric' I will forever think
of the romantic poet as one who sees—with micro-
scopic clarity—that roses *are* garbage heaps." I like
Weingarten's definition of the romantic poet.

Murder in the Good Land

Murder among the creek narrows
and shafts of rice grass, among lacy
coverlets and field sacks, among basement
apple barrels and cellar staples

of onion and beet;
                    beneath piled stones,
razed, broken and scattered stones,
beneath cow bridges, draw bridges, T girders
crossed, and cables, beneath brome, spadefoot,
beneath roots of three-awn
                    and heaven; murder
in the sky between stalks of spikesedge,
between harrier and wolf willow, between
the bedroom walls of formidable sluts
and saints, in the sad blindnesses
of moon and mole, in light as curt
and clearcut as blades of frost
magnified;
                    through blanks of winter wind
through summer soapweed, through welcoming
gates and bolted gates, throughout the blood-rushing
grief of the swarmy sea;
                         murder beside gods
down heathen colonnades, down corridors of scholars
and beggars, down the cathedral colonnades
of orchards in harvest;
                         murder with the clench
of white clover, with the slip of the wandering
tattler, with the slow splash of window
curtains flowing inward
                         with morning air; murder
in the winsome, murder in the wayward,
murder in canyon wrens, in the low beating bell
in the womb, in bone rafters,
                         in mushroom
rings and rosy rings; murder, murder,
murder immortal, pervasive, supreme
everywhere in the good land.

This is the way life on the earth is, and I want to declare that I know it is this way and that knowing it not only doesn't diminish the feelings I've expressed in my poems but adds poignancy and intensity to them, just as I might love an old, well worn and serviceable sweater because it was a gift knit for me by someone I love and who loves me, because it holds history and ancestry in its wrinkles and unique peculiarities and beautiful patterns, and because it belongs to me and I belong to it.

This Nature

Bach is nature, and the Marquis de Sade is nature. Florence Nightingale and the Iron Maiden are nature. Michelangelo's Pietà, the swastika, Penthouse magazine and solar flares are nature. Pedophiles and saints equally are nature. Ash pits, boggy graves, nuclear bombs, tubercle bacillus, Yosemite Falls, abortion, the polio vaccine, all are part of the sum total of everything that is and therefore nature. Nothing that is goes against nature, because nature is the way things are. Nature is what is, everything that is, everything that has been, and everything that is possible, including human actions, inventions, creations, and imaginations. This is my definition. This nature is the nature of roaches and cheetahs and honeysuckle, the nature of a Strauss waltz, the nature of the Ice Ages, the Black Plague, the eruption of Krakatoa, the nature of the slaughter of American bison, the nature of human sacrifice and bloody rituals carried out by Aztecs, Celts, Slavs.

Nothing that exists, including language, is outside nature. We do not know an "outside nature," because knowledge itself is an element of nature. Even the word "unnatural" is part of nature (how could it otherwise be here on this page?) and is therefore self-contradictory.

An ice pick through the chest or a soothing hand on the forehead, both are natural, both gestures of nature. Wild curly dock, malaria, exploding stars, continental drift, and the construction of Hoover Dam are natural, part of what is. Violent birth and violent extinction are older than we are and natural. We know a history of both. We have sometimes been involved in the nature of both. We cannot legitimately use the word "natural" as synonomous with the words "unsullied," "pure," or "righteous."

It is no more against nature for human beings to clearcut a forest than it is against nature for Mt. Vesuvius to erupt and eliminate the town of Herculaneum. Human actions may be judged moral or immoral, wise or unwise, cruel or benevolent, heedless or thoughtful, but those are other terms and other issues. I am speaking of nature. Everything that we name noble is nature, and everything that we name despicable is nature, and our attempt to distinguish between the noble and the despicable is nature.

Calculus, astrophysics, the automobile, the safety pin, and billboards were created by creatures born of the natural world and thus included naturally in the nature of everything that is. If we create justice, it exists in nature. If we act so as to bring compassion into existence, it is real within the natural world. Divinity is of the universe, part of nature, when it is observed and noted and imagined and expressed by creatures born of nature with physical, blood-beating, light-snapping minds. We are thoroughly nature. To claim otherwise is to attempt to place human beings and everything we do in some rare unimaginable realm beyond the universe, thus rendering the power of our origins lost and our obligations vague.

Nature is everything that is. We are not and cannot be "unnatural." Our choices and our actions are never for or against nature. They are always simply of nature. Our decisions then involve determining what it is that we value among this everything-that-is, this nature. What is it we seek to preserve? to eliminate? to modify? to accept? to avoid? to cherish? to respect? to emulate? The decisions we make, how we justify and construct those decisions and the behavior that results, all these become part of the great milieu, and they have their effects in ways we may not always recognize. Our choices and our actions, whether based on aesthetic considerations, moral or spiritual considerations, economic considerations, or rational considerations, must be justified in some way other than by the claim that they are in accord with the natural world; for any behavior, even murder, even suicide, even war, even abuse of the young, can be justified by that claim. We may call these particular acts horrors, but they are horrors that are part of nature, part of everything that is, and they cannot be said to go against nature. They are horrors that are part of nature already replete with horrors. Perhaps these particular acts go against our sense of goodness or compassion, morality or beauty or justice, but they do not go against nature. Annihilation and creation are occurring constantly around us now, and they have occurred always, long before human beings came to be. Nature encompasses all contradictions.

This nature is not a single entity, not a consistent force that sanctions or condemns behavior, not a god-substitute that we can embrace or blame or escape. It composes the entire, complex myriad of ever-changing events and details, unpredictable, paradoxical, passing and eternal, known and mysterious. Nature is the vast expanse of abstractions and multiplicities; it is the void and the concrete presence, an unrestricted inclusiveness. The definition of the word "nature" even includes its own definition and the maker of its definition. It is self-referential.

I deliberately seek out the specific aspects of everything that is that I find ennobling, affirming, that engender in me hope, faith, action, and health, the chaos and mystery that energizes me. I select and cling to them. I choose to value and praise them. Just a few of these aspects, for me, are the words of Shakespeare, Dostoyevsky, Whitman, Melville, Twain, Faulkner, Roethke, Jacob Bronowski, Jesus Christ; the music of Chopin, Beethoven, Bruckner, Anne-Sophie Mutter, the Takacs Quartet; the very existence of the body of preserved art, music, and literature that is my culture; the Magna Carta, the Constitution of the United States and the Bill of Rights; arches, domes, and columns; the grace and order of an NBA basketball game; Jeremy Brett as Sherlock Holmes; the curiosity, facility, and complexity of the human mind that results in the revelations of science; the way sunlight appears—shifting its illuminations and colors on roofs and gardens and fields, making shadows of trees on the curtains—throughout the gradual coming of morning, throughout the patterns of evening, everyday, the gift of morning and evening; snow, that amazement; the surrounding great buffer of stars in which we are immersed; life in its unrelenting, ruthless, self-absorbed, tenacious grasp on being.

We are fortunate as human beings to have the opportunity to discern and to act, to recognize and experience ourselves in this welter of terror and beauty, to add our praise, gratitude, and testimony to the totality of everything that is, to place them as if we were placing seeds in soil into the flux and form of this nature.

———————————

Although research has played a part in the writing of many of my poems, some have come into being *solely because* of research. I find that most research, even the slightest, opens doors of thought for me and offers new, evocative, and interesting vocabulary. I remember being touched upon learning one day that flowers had been found in the graves of the Neanderthals, laid upon the bodies. It seemed to me a revealing gesture toward the mystery of death, indication of an awareness of life and the cessation of life, a recognition of love and loss, a singularly human gesture. I became interested in the ceremonies various cultures have developed to help them deal with death. The poem, "The Dead Never Fight Against Anything," is a product of research into that subject. The actual writing of the poem, as best I can recall it, involved selecting which among the details of these ceremonies would be included in the poem, how they would be ordered, and my effort to state them in a succinct music and a form that could carry my feelings about this subject. The ending was not planned, but it seemed to me to result inevitably from the accumulation of details in the poem.

The Dead Never Fight Against Anything

It's always been that way.
They've allowed themselves to be placed,
knees to chin, in the corners of caves
or in holes in the earth, then covered

with stones; they've let their fingers
be curled around old spears or diadems
or favorite dolls, the stems
of cut flowers.

Whether their skulls were cracked open
and their brains eaten by kin
or whether their brains were pulled
by tongs through their nostrils
and thrown into the dog's dish as waste
are matters that have never concerned them.

They have never offered resistance
to being tied to rocks below the sea,
left for days and nights until their flesh
washed away or likewise to being placed
high in jungle trees or high on scaffolds
alone in the desert until buzzards,
vultures and harpy eagles stripped
their bones bare. They have never minded
jackals nosing at their haunches,
coyotes gnawing at their breasts.

The dead have always been so purely
tolerant. They've let their bones
be rubbed with ointments, ornamented
with ochre, used as kitchen ladles
and spoons. They've been imperturbably
indifferent to the removal of all
their entrails, the resulting cavities
filled with palm wine, aromatic
spices; they have lain complacently
as their abdomens were infused
by syringe with cedar oil.
They've allowed all seven

natural openings of their bodies
to be closed with gold dust.

They've been shrunken and their mouths
sewn shut; they've been wrapped
in gummed linen, corded, bound upright
facing east, hung above coals
and smoked, their ears stuffed
with onions, sent to sea on flaming
pyres. Not one has ever given
a single sign of dissent.

Oblivious to abuse. Even today,
you can hit them and pinch them
and kick them. You can shake them,
scream into their ears. You can cry.
You can kiss them and whisper and moan,
smooth their combed and parted hair, touch
the lips that yesterday spoke, beseech,
entreat with your finest entreaty.
Still, they stare without deviation,
straight into distance and direction.
Old stumps, old shameless logs, rigid
knurls, snow-faced, pitiless,
pitiless betrayal.

Language is one way we have of telling ourselves what
we are experiencing. I believe we not only perceive
but shape and create our experiences by the language
we use to explain them. We experience, in large part,
what we are able to tell ourselves we have experi-
enced. Our experiences *are* the words we choose to
use in describing and thus composing them. Believing

this, it has seemed important to me that poetry func-
tion sometimes to expand the language into areas not
yet penetrated by language, thereby enlarging aware-
ness and experience. I've wanted occasionally to chal-
lenge perceptions that appear to be locked into our
language, for instance, dualities that may not in re-
ality be inevitable—flesh and spirit, analysis and syn-
thesis, inside and outside, cause and effect, life and
death. My intention in a poem, the point of origin of
the poem, often has been simply to take a word or a
concept or an image and stretch its meaning, turning
it upside down and inside out, spinning it around,
taking it to pieces and putting it back together in new
arrangements, to pair seeming contradictions and
make them act as one. Such poems are experiments,
written just to see what happens, what new percep-
tions or ways of thinking might be revealed, what
limitations of perception might be broken.

One afternoon I heard on the radio a rumor that
was circulated about Paganini, the composer, during
his life. What a rumor! I added a few words that
seemed to me to be significant to this rumor, and
then I moved all of these terms around in relation to
one another throughout the poem.

Paganini, and Rumor as Genesis

for John Straley

It could simply have been as reported—
one man going town to town
carrying a hatbox containing the head

of his deceased wife. And thus
the rumors began.

Yet there might actually have been
many men seen in mountain cities
and in cities by the sea, on roads
between, each carrying a hatbox
containing any of several parts
of the deceased: warthog tusk,
deer hoof handle, spiralled pearl
shell of conch, fossil fin of a jawless
fish, moon rock on a silver chain.

Perhaps the rumor began inside
the engraved silver hatbox of the moon
containing many smaller silver hatboxes
inside other silver hatboxes, the last
and smallest, pearl-sized, containing
a naked man standing in the sun, waiting
with ten silver dollars to buy the hat
of a moon for his bald head.

But I think the beginning
really began with one ordinary woman
carrying through town one ordinary
cardboard hatbox containing an average
straw hat, witnessed, however,
as she passed, by a bored, half-moon
visionary of rumors, selling pearl
hatpins on the corner.

A holy man has begun a rumor
asserting that a single hatbox containing
the head of his deceased god is being
passed man to man, town to town,
like a rumor.

In one child's text the final rumor
of genesis begins thusly:

Chapter 1, Verse 1. God rides
disguised as tissue paper in a hatbox,

wrapped ever protective in gentle folds,
like a rose, round and round the velvets,
furs and moon-silver jewels, the bluebirds
and brass whistles, the crinkled foil
butterflies and berry-colored flowers
of a singularly fine chapeau.

Still, if the true beginning were a rumor
telling of a moon-pated man carrying
nothing but his own bible yet unwritten
on the stone skull of his god sealed
inside the perfect holy hatbox not yet
in existence, then there might be
space aplenty for the genesis
of rumors of any kind.

Similarly, when asked to write a short prose piece
on place, I wondered, "Well, what is *place?* What
does that word mean?" I chose an object that seemed
to possess a place, in the traditional sense of the
word, and then tried to investigate that object and
the concept of place in every way I could imagine.

Places within Place

A poplar stands outside the east window of our
upstairs bedroom in the place where I now live,
where I have lived for the past eight years. This
tree has been part of my waking and part of my

sleeping for most of the nights and days of these years. The sound of its leaves turning in the batter of hard rain or wind, or dripping with the fall of lighter moisture, or its branches silent with the rigid silence of zero degrees, have become cadences in my thought and in my thought of possibilities, undercurrents of motion and presence like pulse or breath or passion.

I feel certain that the structure of this poplar against the sky, against the pale of predawn, or catching the sun of dusk, is a factor partially determining the form and pacing of my words, the way I shape the music of my voice, my pleasure in the particular rise and fall of logic or narrative, my interpretation of gesture, my vision of the bones of my stance.

But this tree is not always the same tree. It is not only the poplar of summer and the sharp, craggy poplar of leafless winter, the poplar in snow, encased in ice, the poplar of seeds, full of yellow leaf or with one yellow leaf left, the poplar wounded, leaking dark sap, but it is also the blind poplar I cannot see in fog, the gray and black poplar of night, the white poplar of the moon, the mysterious, rock-shifting subterranean poplar chasing water above the melting core of the earth.

I know it was absolutely not the same tree standing inside the grief of my mother's death as the tree it was outside our window last night during love, as it was a fire rocking with my anger one evening, as it has stood in the way of my hatred, as it has been sharply beautiful with my despair.

And it is also, in truth and actuality, the poplar I imagine it to be, the one possessing a fluttering ghost in each leaf, the messianic poplar suffused with delivered promise, the poplar of a thousand tongues all licking at once inside my ear, the poplar shattered, splintered, and scorched by lightning on the plains before I was born, the poplar I downed with my own ax, the one that fell across my spine and left me face down on the earth.

What is the poplar in the eyes of the June magpie shrieking from its blue branches? What does the poplar become beneath Ursa Major, seven stars on each leaf? Where is the place of the poplar of five years ago, half again as massive? Where precisely *is* the poplar of memory?

What will become of this tree without my designation "poplar," without my announcement of its multiple realities? Devoid of my attentions, is the poplar yet again a different tree? Is it possible to imagine the poplar absent the imagination? If so, then that place might be a new level of the void.

How should we comprehend the place of this particular poplar latched here to this land at this spot and then spun by the earth, carried also by the sun's system, swung round again on the outer rim of the Milky Way galaxy, itself speeding outward? From what place has the poplar come? To what place is it going? Is it necessary to imagine these truths too in order to fully comprehend and appreciate the poplar's present place?

And how does intention interpret this poplar? How does divinity know this tree? What is "benevolence" juxtaposed to a leaf of poplar midsummer?

In one poplar in one moment are a million poplars in a million moments and a million places, places within a place, each singular, each forebearing, each emphatic, all simultaneous in their contradictory and mutually exclusive natures.

How should we define "place"? The word "definition" implies language; the word "place" implies internal and spatial linkages; these then imply one who forges both found and invented connections, which then suggests one who may similarly break, dismiss, reorder, rebuild those connections.

Dare we presume at all to define "poplar"? Dare we presume to define "place"? We do, continually, knowing that we ourselves must always be recognized and included as affected observers within our definitions, as the biased creators of definition, simultaneously shaping and being shaped.

We define, even knowing our definitions will be never ending, never secured, always changing, constantly resisting themselves, constantly determining themselves. This is our burden, and this is our blessing.

The following poem, focusing on the same concept, was written several years before the prose piece.

Nude Standing Alone in the Forest: A Study of Place

In this unattached nudity, the certainty
of her bare feet pressed against the earth—sand-like
soil under the inner arch, essential pine needle
beneath the heel, blessed curl of old leaf—must seem
suddenly crucial. Completely unverified flesh
from the toes up, only the bottoms of her feet
can guess exactly where they are.

Naked for no one, it's obvious that nothing here,
not the noise of the wood warblers or the quiet
of the branch-tip spider or the poised stiffness
of the herb on which it rests, even in the sunlight,
takes particular notice of a bare breast. The wind
doesn't linger, moves steadily to its own places
among the upper leaves of the poplars no matter
what it touches of her on its way. And even outlined
perfectly in white against the background
of yaupon hedges, the curve of her hip and thigh
fitting exactly into their spaces before the wild grape,
her shoulder, as it should, marking the crucial arc
between dogwood and evening, it's still evident
that her body, unacknowledged, doesn't belong.
Uncaressed flesh by itself has no place
but anywhere.

Within this uncertain location of her unfound state,
staring up without a mirror, she can imagine
that she is the sky, as easy and open and accessible,
that her abode, therefore, is heaven.

Or she can believe that she is as undemanding
as the egret disappearing without looking back
over the far shore of the lake, that her habitation,
therefore, is wing. Or she can close her eyes and dream
that she is the motion in the perfect bud of hyacinth
slowly opening its blossom between her legs, petal
by petal to its fullest spread, that the only region
of her desire, therefore, is fantasy.

Yet even without a map it wouldn't be hard
for someone to find her here like this.
It wouldn't be hard for someone to create
the center of her as she creates the focus
of the forest which encircles him. And from
beneath the carefully descending darkness
of someone else, I know she could rise slowly
above all places like a soft, uncovered moon passing
through the thickest branches of the evening
as if the trees had no existence at all. I know
she possesses the power to change every
location of the night, if someone could only
find her inside his own arms right now
and discover where it is that this is so.

    I regard almost all the poems in my book
Legendary Performance as being playful and explor-
atory in this mode, engaged in trying new ways of
perceiving, in challenging old, accepted ways of de-
fining objects, concepts, and attitudes. These poems
center around the activities of a group of fictional
characters—Felicia, Cecil, Sonia, Albert, and
Gordon, and their friends, including Kioka, Naked
Boys on Naked Ponies, Deaf and Blind Beggars,

Felicia's insane uncle who thinks he's a hoary puc-
coon, Cecil's second cousin who can't distinguish be-
tween his memory and his imagination, the dogs,
and others. It was almost pure joy for me to write
these poems. These characters did all the work for
me, asking their own questions, advancing their own
theories, arguing with each other, investigating their
worlds, being bored, being exhilarated. No subject
was ever too ridiculous for them to discuss, no hy-
potheses too absurd for them to advance and debate
seriously. These poems most often begin with a state-
ment, the concept or condition to be explored, such
as the examples below, and then elaborate on that
thought or condition.

Although naked boys and naked ponies
Are definitely two different things, no one has ever
Seen a naked boy off the back of his pony.

from "The Mystery of Union"

Felicia's music teacher gives a concert for Sonia,
Cecil, Albert, Gordon and Felicia and her insane uncle
In the front parlor every holiday season.
After her traditional repertoire she always plays
One piece on her violin in a register so high
The music can't be heard.

from "A Seasonal Tradition"

"The Creation of Sin" began when I was feeling what
Gordon expresses in the first stanza of the poem.
It just struck me that in many ways human beings
are extremely unimaginative, that in our art and lit-
erature we keep investigating the same few human

frailties and sins over and over and over and in the same ways. The poem went off in its own direction from that initial thought.

The Creation of Sin

Gordon wants to commit a sin
Never committed before. He says he is bored
By the lascivious; he has slept through
A thousand adulteries. He calls theft
And murder and greed embarrassingly unimaginative.

He spends an hour each clear afternoon
On the lawn beneath the alders, grooming the dogs,
Trying to imagine a sin so novel
It has not yet been forbidden.

Sometimes, in the moment just before he discerns
The fish treading in light at the bottom
Of the spring or when he studies the eye
Of the short-eared owl in the instant before it sees
The shrew, he is certain he has already committed
That peculiar sin without knowing it. In the early
            morning,
As he watches himself from the icy black cedars
By the window, dreaming in his sleep, he can almost
Define it.

As the sole author of a sin,
Gordon knows he would be obligated to create
Its expiation by himself. Grace by seaside scrutiny,
He might claim, forgiveness by clam classification,
Confession by continual shell collection.
He could invent sacred vows—sworn custodian
Of conifers, promised caretaker of ambush bugs

And toad bugs. He could preach atonement by paper
And mathematics, redemption by ritual
Guessing at the matter of stars.

Today he has recorded a unique grassland prayer
On a tape with the whooping cranes. He has gathered
Sacraments of metamorphic meal moths and
     hardening
Sassafras fruit. And he knows if he could just commit
A truly original sin, it would mean the beginning
Of his only real salvation.

For every poem I've published, I may have tried to write four to five others that were never fully realized. Failures, in other words. And each poem takes many hours of work, failure or not, twenty-five to thirty revisions involving refining, shaping, cutting, and embellishing, reordering logic that seems faulty or unjustified, rewriting language that sounds boring or expected, listening to the music, feeling where the language is heading, trying to follow, wanting the language to surprise me, wanting to please myself.

Some poems begin with a title that intrigues me. I write the poem to find out what the title means, and that's the motivation for the writing. "The Importance of the Whale in the Field of Iris" is such a poem. I don't know where the title came from. It simply occurred to me one day, and I wrote it down. We know how complicated and inexplicable we are as individual human beings. We are constantly perceiving, our bodies taking in and processing sensual information and concurrently affecting that information, our minds debating, formulating, contradicting, playing, dismissing, remembering, on many levels simultaneously. The mind works that way—memories, thoughts, images, facts rising up, many without being consciously recalled or summoned, occasionally coming together in strange juxtapositions, then vanishing quickly. I believe it's important for a writer to latch on to these disappearing words and images, to capture them before they escape. Some may hold the potential for insight or revelation.

The iris is an alluring flower to me. My mother had a beautiful rock garden containing, among many other flowers, iris, and she had a border of iris growing and blooming in the spring along the driveway to our house. As a child, I used to spread the petals of an iris and look down into the blossom. I felt as if I were being drawn into that fragrance and color, everything descending inward. One of my very first poems was titled "I Let the Iris Swallow Me."

I wrote "The Importance of the Whale in the Field of Iris" to try to discover if there was any importance to a whale in a field of iris. Well, to be honest, I wanted an importance to be there, and I worked to find that importance in the poem. The language of the poem and its music helped me to think. That's the key for me.

The Importance of the Whale in the Field of Iris

They would be difficult to tell apart, except
That one of them sails as a single body of flowing

Grey-violet and purple-brown flashes of sun, in and out
Across the steady sky. And one of them brushes
Its ruffled flukes and wrinkled sepals constantly
Against the salt-smooth skin of the other as it swims
        past,
And one of them possesses a radiant indigo moment
Deep beneath its lidded crux into which the curious
Might stare.

In the early morning sun, however, both are equally
Colored and silently sung in orange. And both gather
And promote white prairie gulls which call
And circle and soar about them, diving occasionally
To nip the microscopic snails from their brows.
And both intuitively perceive the patterns
Of webs and courseways, the identical blue-glass
Hairs of connective spiders and blood
Laced across their crystal skin.

If someone may assume that the iris at midnight sways
And bends, attempting to focus the North Star
Exactly at the blue-tinged center of its pale stem,
Then someone may also imagine how the whale rolls
And turns, straining to align inside its narrow eye
At midnight, the bright star-point of Polaris.

And doesn't the iris, by its memory of whale,
Straighten its bladed leaves like rows of baleen
Open in the sun? And doesn't the whale, rising
To the surface, breathe by the cupped space
Of the iris it remembers inside its breast?

If they hadn't been found naturally together,
Who would ever have thought to say: The lunge
Of the breaching whale is the fragile dream

Of the spring iris at dawn; the root of the iris
Is the whale's hard wish for careful hands finding
The earth on their own?

It is only by this juxtaposition we can know
That someone exceptional, in a moment of abandon,
Pressing fresh iris to his face in the dark,
Has taken the whale completely into his heart;
That someone of abandon, in an exceptional moment,
Sitting astride the whale's great sounding spine,
Has been taken down into the quiet heart
Of the iris; that someone imagining a field
Completely abandoned by iris and whale can then see
The absence of an exceptional backbone arching
In purple through dark flowers against the evening sky,
Can see how that union of certainty which only exists
By the heart within the whale within the flower rising
Within the breaching heart within the heart centered
Within the star-point of the field's only buoyant heart
Is so clearly and tragically missing there.

While taking courses in astronomy and zoology as an undergraduate, and meeting my husband, a physicist, at the same time, I not only became intrigued by the cosmological story being told by science, I became exhilarated by it. Scientists today are engaged in exploring all parts of the universe, from elementary particles to new galaxies discovered at distances closer to the beginning of time, from ecological systems in the upper stories of rain forests to tube worms living at warm water clefts at the bottom of the oceans to the beetles of equatorial jungles to bacteria frozen in rocks in Antarctica, from the shifting of the tectonic plates on which our continents rest to the births and deaths of stars, from the dynamics of the brain to genetics and robotics and the color, sound, and motion of computer graphics.

The information derived from these scientific investigations brings to light new mysteries, unique patterns of imagery, new forms of communication opening new arenas of awareness, new structures of thinking, and new stories of the lives of other creatures on earth, the details of which seem simultaneously so alien and yet so familiar. I find the images, the data, the perceptions resulting from these studies revelatory, exciting and bewildering, both affirming and terrifying, and always broadening to the definition of being human. And, for me, the discipline of science provides a balance, a guard against an overly sentimental view of the physical worlds around us, a buffer against destructive superstitions that can lead to fear and false expectations. Science helps to prevent me from claiming that what I *wish* the processes of the universe to be are indeed what they are. I then feel free to value and praise its true majesty. I see no diminishment of the glory of life and being in the contemporary cosmological view. As science reveals more and more detail about the physical universe, the truth of Robert Louis Stevenson's couplet takes on new meaning: "The world is so full of a number of things, / I'm sure we should all be as happy as kings."

Recently I read that the moon is moving away from the earth at the rate of an inch and a half a year, due to the slowing of the earth's rotation. It is just such a small bit of information as this that is not an isolated scientific fact, in my opinion, but one piece of a vision of time and place, a vision of a past and a future of which I am an integral part. What does it mean to realize that in the span of my lifetime I have only a brief glimpse, the shutter opening and closing quickly, of the universe at one moment in its history, the earth and the universe in constant flux, proceeding toward their own demise? What does it mean to the heart, to a sense of justice, for example, to realize that the earth, once begun on its quick spinning, immediately began to slow, the sun to die, the moon to move away? In light of these facts, what does it mean to act honorably? How is the definition of integrity, of hope, affected?

To assimilate such facts, as well as other parts of this science-based cosmological vision, and to try to interpret them in their beauty and fearsomeness, is something I've wanted to do in my poetry. I knew I wanted to try to do this early in my writing years. Without artistic expression, any fact remains alien, unpossessed, with no reverberation in the soul. I wanted to try to find ways to absorb our contemporary cosmology with all of its implications and to infuse it with spiritual meaning, to discover its spiritual attributes. It has seemed to me impossible to live in our world, to survive—the split, the rending being too great—if a union could not be found and created between these two ways of knowing, the artistic and the scientific, both so essential and so present in our lives. I believe the union is there and only lacks adequate expression to bring it into reality.

I consider the following poem to be one expression of evolution. The poem began with its title, "The Family Is All There Is." In the writing of the poem I wanted to establish the truth of the title within my definition of "family," presenting evidence, truthful and emotional evidence. I was asked by the editor of the journal to which I first submitted this poem to rethink the original ending. I am grateful to that editor, because I did rewrite the ending to include the list in the last, long stanza, and I also thought very, very carefully about whether to keep the last line. I decided in its favor.

The Family Is All There Is

Think of those old, enduring connections
found in all flesh—the channeling
wires and threads, vacuoles, granules,
plasma and pods, purple veins, ascending
boles and coral sapwood (sugar-
and light-filled), those common ligaments,
filaments, fibers and canals.

Seminal to all kin also is the open
mouth—in heart urchin and octopus belly,
in catfish, moonfish, forest lily,
and rugosa rose, in thirsty magpie,
wailing cat cub, barker, yodeler,
yawning coati.

And there is a pervasive clasping
common to the clan—the hard nails
of lichen and ivy sucker
on the church wall, the bean tendril
and the taproot, the bolted coupling
of crane flies, the hold of the shearwater
on its morning squid, guanine
to cytosine, adenine to thymine,
fingers around fingers, the grip
of the voice on presence, the grasp
of the self on place.

Remember the same hair on pygmy
dormouse and yellow-necked caterpillar,
covering red baboon, thistle seed
and willow herb? Remember the similar
snorts of warthog, walrus, male moose
and sumo wrestler? Remember the familiar
whinny and shimmer found in river birches,
bay mares and bullfrog tadpoles,
in children playing at shoulder tag
on a summer lawn?

The family—weavers, reachers, winders
and connivers, pumpers, runners, air
and bubble riders, rock-sitters, wave-gliders,
wire-wobblers, soothers, flagellators—all
brothers, sisters, all there is.

Name something else.

A geologist friend of mine once mentioned to me
the poem "The Voice of the Precambrian Sea," an-
other poem incorporating the concept of evolution.
He said to me, "I love the earth. I just love the earth.

It's so . . . so. . . ." I said, "So voluptuous?" And he said, "So . . . so ancestral, so comedic." I like those words put together—the earth, ancient relative, living and lively.

The Voice of the Precambrian Sea

During the dearth and lack of those two thousand
Million years of death, one wished primarily
Just to grasp tightly, to compose, to circle,
To link and fasten skillfully, as one
Crusty grey bryozoan builds upon another,
To be *anything* particular, flexing and releasing
In controlled spasms, to make boundaries—replicating
Chains, membranes, epitheliums—to latch on with
    power
As hooked mussels now adhere to rocky beaches;
To roll up tightly, fistlike, as a water possum,
Spine and skin, curls against the cold;
To become godlike with transformation.

And in that time one eventually wished,
With the dull swell and fall of the surf, to rise up
Out of oneself, to move straight into the violet
Billowing of evening as a willed structure of flight
Trailing feet, or by six pins to balance
Above the shore on a swollen blue lupine, tender,
Almost sore with sap, to shimmer there,
Specific and alone, two yellow wings
Like splinters of morning.

One yearned simultaneously to be invisible,
In the way the oak toad is invisible among
The ashy debris of the scrub-forest floor;

To be grandiose as deserts are grandiose
With punctata and peccaries, Joshua tree,
Saguaro and the mule-ears blossom; to be precise
As the long gleaming hairs of the gourami, swaying
And touching, find the moss and roughage
Of the pond bottom with precision; to stitch
And stitch (that dream) slowly and exactly
As a woman at her tapestry with needle and thread
Sews each succeeding canopy of the rain forest
And with silver threads creates at last
The shining eyes of the capuchins huddled
Among the black leaves of the upper branches.

One longed to be able to taste the salt
Of pity, to hold by bones the stone of grief,
To take in by acknowledgment the light
Of spring lilies in a purple vase, five white
Birds flying before a thunderhead, to become
Infinite by reflection, announcing out loud
In one's own language, by one's own voice,
The fabrication of these desires, this day
Of their recitation.

I believe that the expansion of human awareness to include our current knowledge of the heavens, the bodies and the origins inhabiting those spaces, is a form of liberty.

Consider, for example, the images and information being gathered by the Hubble Space Telescope. The following is taken from text accompanying an image found on the internet.

Embedded in this Hubble Space Telescope image of nearby and distant galaxies are 18 young galaxies or galactic building blocks, each containing dust, gas, and a few billion stars. Each of these objects is 11 billion light-years from Earth. . . . At this distance, the universe was only about 16 percent of its current age. . . . The faintest objects visible in this image are 2 billion times fainter than what the unaided eye can see from a dark location on Earth.

I find our awareness of the distances and times through which our earth is moving liberating because this knowledge enlarges the range of human experience and because that range is enormous in its mystery. We could all rest and recline in blissful anonymity in that encompassing mystery.

Achieving Perspective

Straight up away from this road,
Away from the fitted particles of frost
Coating the hull of each chick pea,
And the stiff archer bug making its way
In the morning dark, toe hair by toe hair,
Up the stem of the trillium,
Straight up through the sky above this road right now,
The galaxies of the Cygnus A cluster
Are colliding with each other in a massive swarm
Of interpenetrating and exploding catastrophes.
I try to remember that.

And even in the gold and purple pretense
Of evening, I make myself remember
That it would take 40,000 years full of gathering

Into leaf and dropping, full of pulp splitting
And the hard wrinkling of seed, of the rising up
Of wood fibers and the disintegration of forests,
Of this lake disappearing completely in the bodies
Of toad slush and duckweed rock,
40,000 years and the fastest thing we own,
To reach the one star nearest to us.

And when you speak to me like this,
I try to remember that the wood and cement walls
Of this room are being swept away now,
Molecule by molecule, in a slow and steady wind,
And nothing at all separates our bodies
From the vast emptiness expanding, and I know
We are sitting in our chairs
Discoursing in the middle of the blackness of space.
And when you look at me
I try to recall that at this moment
Somewhere millions of miles beyond the dimness
Of the sun, the comet Biela, speeding
In its rocks and ices, is just beginning to enter
The widest arc of its elliptical turn.

The Delight of Being Lost

There are times when one might wish to be nothing
but the plain crease and budded nipple
of a breast, nothing but the manner in the lay
of an arm across a pillow or the pressure of hips
and shoulders on a sheet. Sometimes there is a desire
to draw down into the dull turn of the inner knee,
    dumb
and isolated from the cognizant details of any summer
    night,

to be chin and crotch solely as the unrecorded, passing
moments of themselves, to have no name or place but
        breath.

If wished enough, it might be possible to sink away
        completely,
to leave the persistent presence of pine trees
brushing against the eaves, loons circling the lake,
making an issue of direction; to sink away, remaining
awake inside the oblivion deep within a naked thigh,
to open the eyes inside the blindness of a wrist, hearing
nothing but the deafness in the curve of the neck.

It would seem a perfect joy to me tonight
to lie still in this darkness, to deny everything
but the rise in the line of ankle or spine, ignoring
the angles of walls establishing definable spaces,
ignoring the clear, moon-shadow signals of specific
circumstance, to recognize no reality but the universal
anonymity of a particular body which might then be
        stroked
and kissed and fondled and worshipped without ever
        knowing
or caring to ask by whom or where or how it was given
such pleasure.

I'm often enamored with the thought that our
bodies are made from the dust of old stars, another
story that's part of our current cosmology. I'm fond
of thinking to myself, "If the body is made from the
dust of old stars, then just imagine where it has been,
all the realms through which it has traveled, all the
forms it has assumed. Could it even at one time have
given forth light itself? Think of everything it has

experienced. How old and how wise it must be in many ways."

A Self-Analysis of Dust

We know something about dust here on earth.
It makes its visible home in shafts of sunlight.
It can scatter unpredictably and float
in particles without wings. It can't be caught by
     hand.
It can find the tiny throats of every beggarweed
along the road. It can become the detectable funnel
of the wind. Sometimes dust can be gold.

Some people say dust represents the end,
the paltry evidence of a final dissolution.
It is considered a symbol of desertion when it lies
in long, empty corridors, a proof of degenerate
vacancy when it covers rose damask settees.
Its essence, as a result, is occasionally linked
with cold ashes.

But some say dust is the beginning,
its slow accumulation and eventual density in space
resulting in the formation of great rolling nebulae,
in the emergence of expansive galactic clusters,
the collapse of heavy stars into themselves. Dust,
in the right circumstances, can make its own light.
Some say our bodies are composed of the dust
of old stars, our minds are made from the dust
of old stars born and disintegrated billions
of years ago.If the atoms of our brains have
already experienced that beginning and that end,
if they have already accomplished that generation

of light, have already circumnavigated those far
reaches of blackness separated and alone, then
what vision is it we must always have seen
without realizing yet that we do?

Some people even believe that a measure of dust
of any kind, when blown upon by the proper breath,
can become a living soul. I wonder what soul
might be created if the light from a billion bright stars
were to be carefully gathered and measured
and blown upon here by living dust.

A few people are certain by the light
of their own minds and souls that dust knows
no time, being the one pure synthesis
of the beginning and the end.

When writing, I respect the body and pay close
attention to all that it knows, in what directions it
leads me, to what it responds quickly and forcefully,
to the music and cadences that entice it. The body
and its sensuality are the only forces that can truly
fill and quicken the otherwise inert framework of
words and sentences on the page.

———————

And speaking of bodies . . . I've written many love
poems, for many reasons. Sexual love, as we know so
well, is overwhelming, so obsessive. Why? Why do
we give ourselves in this way for a few moments, not
only to one another, but somehow to something else,
losing ourselves, merging momentarily into some-
thing grander and larger? I believe we're drawn back

to sexual union again and again, because in those few moments of intimacy, we gain an insight into something vitally important, especially if we are with someone with whom we share histories and compassions and mutual reverences. And then we lose that insight. We want to find it again, to be one with it again. "When At Night" was an attempt to capture the expansive nature I feel is inherent to sexual love, the way, during those moments, we move outward in generosity and identity to meet all elements of the universe. The title comes from a song sung in Humperdinck's opera *Hansel and Gretel:* "When at night I go to sleep / Fourteen angels watch do keep."

When At Night

Suppose all of you came in the dark,
each one, up to my bed while I was sleeping;

Suppose one of you took my hand
without waking me and touched my fingers,
moved your lips the length of each one, down
into the crotch with your tongue and up again,
slowly sucking the nipple of each knuckle
with your eyes closed;

Suppose two of you were at my head, the breath
of one in my ear like a bird/moth thuddering
at a silk screen; the other fully engaged, mouth
tasting of sweet meats and liquors,
kissing my mouth;

Suppose another drew the covers
down to my feet, slipped the loops

from the buttons, spread my gown,
ministering mouth again around the dark
of each breast, pulling and puckering
in the way that water in a stir
pulls and puckers a fallen
bellflower into itself;

Two at my shoulders to ease
the gown away, take it down
past my waist and hips, over my ankles
to the end of the bed; one of you
is made to adore the belly; one of you
is obsessed with dampness; at my bent
knees now, another watching, at my parted
thighs another; and one to oversee
the separation and one to guard the joining
and one to equal my trembling and one
to protect my moaning;

And at dawn, if everything were put
in place again, closing, sealing, my legs
together, straight, the quilt folded
and tucked to my chin; if all of you
stepped back, away, into your places,
into the translucence of glass
at the window, into the ground breezes
swelling the limber grasses, into the river
of insect rubbings below the field and the light
expanding the empty spaces of the elm, back
into the rising black of the hawk deepening
the shallow sky, and we all woke then
so much happier than before, well,
there wouldn't be anything
wrong in that, would there?

"The Hummingbird: A Seduction" began because I was enchanted with the courtship ritual the male hummingbird performs in order to seduce the female. I've always been amused and delighted with all the extremes that so many male animals go to in order to win the attention and cooperation of females, all of the courtship displays, extravagant plumages, the dances, calls and songs, the raucous contests, territorial squabblings, blusterings and boastings. The intensity and invention occurring at those times seem to confirm and bolster my belief that there's something extremely vital, affirming, and transfiguring happening during sexual union, something more than procreation, although that alone is pretty glorious. Sexual union, coming with love and compassion, is too beautiful, too full of light and energy, its visionary possibilities too great, to be simply a mechanical act. I could be wrong, but I believe this, and such was the impetus for this poem.

The Hummingbird: A Seduction

If I were a female hummingbird perched still
And quiet on an upper myrtle branch
In the spring afternoon and if you were a male
Alone in the whole heavens before me, having parted
Yourself, for me, from cedar top and honeysuckle stem
And earth down, your body hovering in midair
Far away from jewelweed, thistle and bee balm;

And if I watched how you fell, plummeting before me,
And how you rose again and fell, with such mastery
That I believed for a moment *you* were the sky

And the red-marked bird diving inside your
    circumference
Was just the physical revelation of the light's
Most perfect desire;

And if I saw your sweeping and sucking
Performance of swirling egg and semen in the air,
The weaving, twisting vision of red petal
And nectar and soaring rump, the rush of your wing
In its grand confusion of arcing and splitting
Created completely out of nothing just for me,

Then when you came down to me, I would call you
My own spinning bloom of ruby sage, my funneling
Storm of sunlit sperm and pollen, my only breathless
Piece of scarlet sky, and I would bless the base
Of each of your feathers and touch the tine
Of string muscles binding your wings and taste
The odor of your glistening oils and hunt
The honey in your crimson flare
And I would take you and take you and take you
Deep into any kind of nest you ever wanted.

I know that the audience I envision for my poetry is
crucial to determining what the poem-in-progress
eventually becomes. This is a subtle issue for me, be-
cause I don't explicitly define the audience to my-
self. I'm not always conscious of how I'm
envisioning my audience, and the audience is not al-
ways the same. What I am very certain of, however,
is that the audience to whom I imagine I'm speaking
will determine to a great extent the freedom and
originality the language achieves, the expanse of its

investigative reach, the breadth of its whimsy, its willingness to take risks with concepts and voices and to challenge traditional views, the stance and tone it adopts.

In several of my early poems, I am simply talking to myself, directing myself, "Consider this. . . . Imagine it this way. . . ." In other poems, I'm speaking to a lover (that's usually obvious), in others to my conception of a respected editor, the receptive, knowledgeable, astute, and demanding reader. Sometimes I'm addressing the best part of myself, the person I wish I could be. I want to create that person by means of the poem, to allow the poem to create that person. In other poems I feel I'm speaking to a benevolence, one who is wishing, longing, for our goodness. I'm addressing that generosity responsible for the astonishing intricacy, the complexity in order and chaos of the worlds I see surrounding me, the coming realization of that inventive power. I don't often directly address this essence but imagine such a presence receiving my poem.

And many times the audience I envision is some part of all of these at once.

I asked myself one day, "What is the grandest gift we receive?" I didn't know the answer but found one as I wrote the poem.

The Greatest Grandeur

Some say it's in the reptilian dance
of the purple-tongued sand goanna,
for there the magnificent translation

of tenacity into bone and grace occurs.

And some declare it to be an expansive
desert—solid rust-orange rock
like dusk captured on earth in stone—
simply for the perfect contrast it provides
to the blue-grey ridge of rain
in the distant hills.

Some claim the harmonics of shifting
electron rings to be most rare and some
the complex motion of seven sandpipers
bisecting the arcs and pitches of come
and retreat over the mounting hayfield.

Others, for grandeur, choose the terror
of lightning peals on prairies or the tall
collapsing cathedrals of stormy seas,
because there they feel dwarfed
and appropriately helpless; others select
the serenity of that ceiling/cellar
of stars they see at night on placid lakes,
because there they feel assured
and universally magnanimous.

But it is the dark emptiness contained
in every next moment that seems to me
the most singularly glorious gift,
that void which one is free to fill
with processions of men bearing burning
cedar knots or with parades of blue horses,
belled and ribboned and stepping sideways,
with tumbling white-faced mimes or companies
of black-robed choristers; to fill simply
with hammered silver teapots or kiln-dried
crockery, tangerine and almond custards,

polonaises, polkas, whittling sticks, wailing
walls; that space large enough to hold all
invented blasphemies and pieties, 10,000
definitions of god and more, never fully
filled, never.

I had originally written a dedication for this poem. I
forgot about it and only found it again recently. It's
an indication of the audience I imagined as I was
writing.

For that power which gives as gift
the inestimable emptiness, the vast
unfillable void contained
in every next moment.

———————

And I write because I have an obligation to give
something back for all of the gifts that have been
given to me. I am aware that the circumstances of my
life, the place and times in which I have lived, are not
only unique in human history but extremely blessed.
I realize I have been spared many of the fears, anxiet-
ies, uncertainties, and sufferings that most other
human beings of other cultures and times have expe-
rienced and that many people in the world are expe-
riencing today. Here in the United States during the
latter half of the twentieth century, even coming
from a lower middle-class family, I have always been
clothed, always been fed, kept warm and dry, have
been skillfully cared for after injury, in sickness, and
during childbirth, have been protected against many

fatal or crippling diseases, as have my children, have always had safe and comfortable shelter, have never feared marauders, have never been routed from my home or experienced the plights of a refugee, have never witnessed firsthand the horrors of war, was never abused as a child, was offered education by kind teachers from the age of five through graduate school. And my adult life has been blessed with a resilient and stable government, the freedom to write and publish, a dynamic culture of arts and sciences, a loving and talented husband, two fine, healthy sons, and with funds and leisure time for travel, reading, and entertainments of many varieties.

I want to try to be worthy of these blessings, to give as I have been given to and as I have received, to express my appreciation for all those living before me, many, many generations of people, who have worked to contribute to the full and varied culture it has been my privilege to enjoy.

I believe something magical happens during the acts of giving and receiving, something extremely important and life engendering. The giver gives and receives through the act of giving and thereby undergoes an emboldening change. The receiver receives and gives through the act of receiving and thereby is altered in significant ways. Without giving, without offering thanks and hoping for that offering to be received, I believe one part of who we could be might never come into existence, might never be realized—that state during which the blood courses more brilliantly, the senses strengthen and increase,

possibilities expand, and new light comes to sing in
the bones.

The Gift of Reception

There is great kindness in reception.
Arthur, stretched still and stomach-flat,
is grateful for the wild guinea hen
who finally comes out of the willow to take
from his hand. There is a compliment
in the acceptance of that offering.

Some people believe they actually become the gift
they present, the spirit being united with the jade
figurine or caught circling in the silver ring
in its velvet case. Self-identity can be disguised
and presented as a lacquered mahogany box, a lace
shawl. If an ivory pendant or a grouping of wild
pinks and asters can become the physical
representation of the soul, then Cain,
Cain had valid motive.

Don't you understand that if you lie still,
if you take what I discover of your body,
if you accept what my fingertips can present to you
of your own face, how I might become what I give,
and how, by this investment, I might be bound
to keep seeking you forever?

This morning I want to give back the steep and rocky
ledge of this cold oak forest. I want to give back
the dense haze deepening further into frost
and the tight dry leaves scratching in the higher
cold. I want to give back my identity caught

in the expanding dimension of quiet found
by the jay. And with my soul disguised
as the wide diffusion of the sun behind the clouds,
I want to give back the conviction that light
is the only source of itself. I want these gifts
to be taken. I want to be invested in the one
who accepts them.

Maybe the most benevolent angel we can know
is the one whose body lies receptive, composed
of all the gifts we want most to give.

The giving of praise is one activity that humans can do very well. I don't *believe* we can praise, I *know* we can praise. Even in our ignorance and confusion, we can praise very beautifully and in an astonishing variety of ingenious ways. Poetry, in its seeking and questing, in its notice and naming, is one means of giving praise. It's my way.

Supposition

Suppose the molecular changes taking place
In the mind during the act of praise
Resulted in an emanation rising into space.
Suppose that emanation went forth
In the configuration of its occasion:
For instance, the design of rain pocks
On the lake's surface or the blue depths
Of the canyon with its horizontal cedars stunted.

Suppose praise had physical properties
And actually endured? What if the pattern
Of its disturbances rose beyond the atmosphere,

Becoming a permanent outline implanted in the
      cosmos—
The sound of the celebratory banjo or horn
Lodging near the third star of Orion's belt;
Or to the east of the Pleiades, an atomic
Disarrangement of the words,
"How particular, the pod-eyed hermit crab
And his prickly orange legs"?

Suppose benevolent praise,
Coming into being by our will,
Had a separate existence, its purple or azure light
Gathering in the upper reaches, affecting
The aura of morning haze over autumn fields,
Or causing a perturbation in the mode of an asteroid.
What if praise and its emanations
Were necessary catalysts to the harmonious
Expansion of the void? Suppose, for the prosperous
Welfare of the universe, there were an element
Of need involved.

———————

In Order to Perceive

At first you see nothing. The experience is similar
To opening your eyes wide as white marbles
Inside the deepest cave, beneath tons of limestone,
Or being awake in a dark room, your head
Under a heavy blanket.

Then someone suggests there is a single candle
Wavering far off in one corner, flickering red.
You think you see it
As someone else draws your attention to the sharp
Beaming wing tips, the white end of the beak,

The obvious three points of the wild goose overhead
And the seven-starred poinsettia to the west, the bright
Cluster at its belly.

You are able to recognize, when you are shown,
The sparks flying from the mane of the black stallion,
The lightning of his hooves as he rears,
And in the background a thick forest spreading
To the east, each leaf a distinct pinprick of light.

Then you begin to notice things for yourself,
A line of torches curving along a black valley,
A sparkling flower, no bigger than a snowflake,
Shining by itself in the northwest coordinate.
It is you who discovers the particular flash
Of each tooth inside the bear's open mouth and the
        miners
With their lighted helmets rising in a row.

How clear and explicit, you tell someone with
        confidence,
That ship, each separate gleaming line of its rigging,
The glowing dots of the oars, the radiating
Eyes of the figure on the prow, the corners
Of each sail lit.

Soon there is no hesitation to the breadth
Of your discoveries. Until one night during the long
Intensity of your observation, you look so perfectly
That you finally see yourself, off in the distance
Among the glittering hounds and hunters, beside the
        white
Shadows of the swans. There are points of fire
At your fingertips, a brilliance at the junctures
Of your bones. You watch yourself floating,

Your heels in their orbits, your hair spreading
Like a phosphorescent cloud, as you rise slowly,
A skeleton of glass beads, above the black desert,
Over the lanterned hillsides and on out through the
    hollow
Stretching directly overhead.

The questions of who we are and why we are here, what self-consciousness is, how we might come to see and know ourselves, have been with me in some form since childhood. As a child, I used to put myself to sleep sometimes by wondering who I was, and why I was who I was, and why I was Pattiann Tall and not someone else, and who the I was who was asking these questions. (This exercise would undoubtedly put anyone to sleep quickly.)

When I was four or five years old, I remember saying to my mother that I knew I would never be able to see what I looked like with my eyes closed. She suggested that she take my picture with my eyes closed and then I could see. We did that. I have the photograph. I'm sitting on a stoop in our backyard wearing a sweater and matching beret my mother knit for me. I'm holding on my lap a little gypsy doll, a gift from my dad, a fortune-teller doll with a crystal ball. I'm smiling and have my eyes closed. I remember this event well. This was my way, at the time, of wondering about self and existence, about perception and perception of self and concept of self. What a kind, wise, gracious mother not to laugh or ignore my remark but to honor it, to encourage investigation of such questions and to address them seriously.

This quest for self-knowledge, for an understanding of how we perceive and what obligations come with self-awareness, is at the center of most of my poems.

In my poems, I have often tried to investigate the nature of the divine, to find and to express a divinity, to discover how divinity comes into being, what role humans might play in that creation, how I might recognize divinity. These have seemed to me questions of ultimate concern. The following is a prose examination of the structure of divinity, of the sacred and the holy.

Surprised by the Sacred

Driving on a paved road not far from my home last summer, I saw an injured snake, hit by a car, stuck by its open wound to the road. It was curling and writhing, struggling to free itself. I stopped and went back, thinking to move it from the hot, bare road and into the shade and shelter of the weeded ditch where I felt it would eventually die, yet possibly suffer a little less.

As I reached the snake lying on its back, twisted around its wound, and bent to move it, it took one very sharp, deep breath, a gasp so deep I could see its ribcage rise beneath the ivory scales along its upper body, and, in that moment, it died. It lay suddenly without moving, not at all the existence it had been, inexorably altered in being. And its gasp and the dying were simultaneous, the breath stopped, held within the narrow width of its dead body forever.

I was stunned in that moment by an awareness of order and union: the snake at my fingertips had been a living creature, drawing breath as I draw breath, taking air into its body. I had witnessed that breath. "Living"—the word was suddenly expanded for me in meaning, in impact. It now embodied a compassion of connection wider, more undeniable than any I had perceived before.

One definition of sacred is: declared holy. I would declare this moment to be a sacred moment in my life, and I would declare the elements composing this moment—the struggling snake, its life ceasing, the vision of its breathing, the unrelenting summer sun, the steady buzz and burr of the insects in the weeds around us, the fragrance of dry grasses—all these elements I would declare to be holy in their bearing of essence and divinity.

A similar moment of enlightenment, also involving a snake, is described in a poem by D. H. Lawrence. On a hot summer day the speaker of the poem comes upon a snake drinking at his water-trough.

> He sipped with his straight mouth,
> Softly drank through his straight gums,
>   into his slack long body,
> Silently.
>
> . . . .
>
> He lifted his head from his drinking, as
>   cattle do,
>
> . . . .
>
> And flickered his two-forked tongue from
>   his lips, and mused a moment,
> And stooped and drank a little more,

As the speaker watches, he believes the snake is poisonous and that he should kill it.

But must I confess how I liked him,
How glad I was he had come like a guest
    in quiet, to drink at my water-trough
And depart peaceful, pacified, and
    thankless,
Into the burning bowels of this earth?

The underlying unity of life is revealed in that moment. All life—beautiful or reprehensible, dangerous or benign—takes sustenance from the earth, all lips that drink, all throats and bodies and roots that seek water.

And all forms of life are one in their tenacity, in their determined grip on existence, in their unfaltering will-to-be, exhibited so obviously in the sow thistle rising through any crevice forced or found in cement or rock; in mayweed and burdock thriving along roadsides, among rubbish and waste; in the unrelenting persistence of birds—sparrows, crows, warblers—up at dawn, even after a sudden spring storm of sleet and ice, a long frigid night, calling and scrabbling in the cold, there to survive, crisis or no. "Urge and urge and urge / Always the procreant urge of the world," Walt Whitman writes in "Song of Myself."

This kinship of being, of devotion to life, once recognized, demands respect for each living entity in its place. Another definition of sacred is: venerable, worthy of respect.

My family moved to a farm in Missouri when I was fifteen. Along with the purchase of the farm, we inherited a herd of sheep, just at lambing season. It was a painfully cold, late January, and when twins were born, it was often necessary to bring one lamb into the house to keep it from freezing while the ewe mother took care of the other. Even today, many years later, I can see those newborn lambs, whiter and cleaner than the snow they lay on at birth, each so immediately out of the warm, wet womb into the wide winter cold, the unfathomably deep, grey skies, the world wholly new to their eyes just opened, and, hanging from each lamb, the drying string of a bloody umbilical cord.

I've never felt anything again so soft as the fleecy silk of those young lambs, silk so soft it was barely discernible against my fingertips, the sensation enhanced by the feel of the thin, warm body beating beneath. I remember having one of my fingers accidentally mistaken for a nipple and taken quickly into a lamb's mouth, the surprisingly strong sucking and gripping power of that tongue and throat on my finger. Life is this final, the altogether everything, this crucial.

We seem to be creatures who need physical sensation, tangible objects to imbue with the abstractions that mean so much to us as a species—innocence, compassion, peace. Each of the newborn lambs we cared for during those early years of my adolescence has come to be for me the very feel, the sound, the living body of faith, of purity and hope. These are the same virtues many people in the past believed were presented to God in the sacrifice of un-blemished lambs. "Behold the Lamb of God," John the Baptist announces when he sees Christ walking toward him out of the crowd. The newborn lambs of my adolescence entered the world bearing this history in their being, in their bodies, stories of the sacred. And they were dear to me, their presence enhanced, be-cause of the stories they bore.

The surprise of encountering unusual jux-tapositions can also bring awareness of the di-vine carnival of life, this sacred circus that surrounds us—the juxtaposition of a tomcat sleeping with a fallen forsythia blossom on his head, a toad found in the toe of a rubber boot, the disappearing and ephemeral form of surf blown against implacable rock, the wild aban-don and indifference of nature seen against the static of the manmade. . . .

> Out from the hollow
> of Great Buddha's nose—
> comes a swallow!
>
> *Issa*

Or the vast and the far seen clearly against the small and the near. . . .

> A lovely thing to see:
> through the paper window's hole
> the Galaxy.
>
> *Issa*

Once, in a muddy, ill-smelling chicken yard noisy with cackling hens, I held in my hand one half of a fertilized chicken egg accidentally broken. In the center of that half shell filled with golden yolk, a small dot of bright blood pulsed regularly and steadily into a threaded network of spreading red webs so small and fine they were hardly visible in their reality. Heart and its pathways.

For a moment I was lifted out of that scene. Everything around me disappeared, and nothing existed except that vibrant red instant of complex life proceeding, though doomed, with astonishing trust. The miracle of it, a hallowed miracle. Who could think otherwise?

". . . a mouse is miracle enough to stagger sextillions of infidels," Whitman, again, from "Song of Myself." And I agree.

I've often experienced a moment of deep happiness when watching someone sleeping, and wondered why. I think what occasions that joy is an awareness of the truth that the body itself is totally innocent, flesh and bone unquestionably fine, justified and without blame. All aspects—feet and legs, the intricacy of the ears, the grace of the neck and the arms—all are sculptures unsurpassed in beauty of line and function. And the hands, solely in and of themselves, are astonishingly perfect and inviolate. Jacob Bronowski writes in *The Ascent of Man:*

> I remember as a young father tiptoeing
> to the cradle of my first daughter when
> she was four or five days old, and
> thinking, "These marvellous fingers,

every joint so perfect, down to the finger nails. I could not have designed that detail in a million years."

When the human body is sleeping we can see clearly, without interference or confusion, that the body is indeed sacred and honorable, a grand gift we hold in trust. It is sublime and chaste in its loveliness and as unbothered by greed or violence, by deceit or guilt, as a brilliantly yellow cottonwood standing in an autumn field, as the moon filling the boundaries of its white stone place. If there is sin, it resides elsewhere. "The man's body is sacred and the woman's body is sacred . . ." (Whitman, "I Sing the Body Electric").

I believe the world provides every physical image and sensation we will ever need in order to experience the sacred, to declare the holy, if we could only learn to recognize it, if we could only hone and refine our sense of the divine, just as we learn to see and distinguish with accuracy the ant on the trunk of the poplar, the Pole Star in Ursa Minor, rain coming toward us on the wind; just as we come to identify the sounds we hear, the voices of our children, the creak of the floor at the lover's footstep, the call of a finch unseen in the top of a pine; just as we can detect and name the scent of cedar or sage, wild blackberries or river mud and rotting logs.

Might it be possible, if we try, to become so attuned to the divine that we are able to perceive and announce it with such ease too? And perhaps the divine, the sacred, the holy, only come into complete existence through our witness of them, our witness for them and to them. Perhaps reciprocal creation, as I observe it operating in my own writing—creating the poem which simultaneously creates me which simultaneously creates the poem coming into being—just as the marsh wren created by the marsh simultaneously creates and dreams the marsh of its creation and therefore creates itself—is the same phenomenon occurring in regard to divinity. Maybe the existence of divinity in the universe depends in part on us. We may be the consciousness of the universe, the way by which it can come to see and love and honor itself. If this is so, then our obligations are mighty and humbling. We are cocreators. We are servants.

I believe we move through the sacred constantly, yet remain oblivious to its presence except during those rare, unexpected moments when we are suddenly shocked and shaken awake, compelled to perceive and acknowledge. During those brief moments we know with bone-centered conviction who it is we are; with breath-and-pulse clarity where it is we have come from; and with earth-solid certainty we know to what it is we owe all our allegiance, all our heart, all our soul, all our love.

I want to be both seeker and believer simultaneously, maintaining a balance between the two, believing in those concepts that generate strength, faith, hope, and gratitude, while at the same time continuing to question with imagination and curiosity the state of being human in a world of terrifying magnificence and beauty.

In my poems I've asked questions about god, that essence, that benevolence, that presence so many human beings have sensed to be part of our experience, a presence essential to our definition of ourselves and our obligations, and yet so elusive. "I hear and behold God in every object, yet understand God not in the least," Walt Whitman writes in "Song of Myself." I consider my poems on this subject to be explorations, experiments, suppositions, offerings to that mystery moving toward righteous completion, that grace evolving toward fulfillment, the receiver, the giver of life, "the pattern that both theologians and physicists call God" (Barry Lopez), the "Master of beauty, craftsman of the snowflake, / inimitable contriver, / endower of Earth so gorgeous & different from the boring Moon" (John Berryman), the "*in* you is the presence that / will be, when all the stars are dead" (Rilke).

I want my poems that explore the essence of god and divinity to incorporate the best of all that I am able to bring to any poem. In my inadequacy and ignorance, I hope they contain my grateful thanks, my ceaseless curiosity and steady faith, my compassion and reverence for the universe in all of its manifestations and creations.

The Possible Suffering of a God During Creation

It might be continuous—the despair he experiences
Over the imperfection of the unfinished, the weaving
Body of the imprisoned moonfish, for instance,
Whose invisible arms in the mid-waters of the deep sea
Are not yet free, or the velvet-blue vervain
Whose grainy tongue will not move to speak, or the ear
Of the spitting spider still oblivious to sound.

It might be pervasive—the anguish he feels
Over the falling away of everything that the duration
Of the creation must, of necessity, demand, maybe
    feeling
The break of each and every russet-headed grass
Collapsing under winter ice or feeling the split
Of each dried and brittle yellow wing of the sycamore
As it falls from the branch. Maybe he winces
At each particle-by-particle disintegration of the
    limestone
Ledge into the crevasse and the resulting compulsion
Of the crevasse to rise grain by grain, obliterating itself.

And maybe he suffers from the suffering
Inherent to the transitory, feeling grief himself
For the grief of shattered beaches, disembodied bones
And claws, twisted squid, piles of ripped and tangled,
Uprooted turtles and rock crabs and Jonah crabs,
Sand bugs, seaweed and kelp.

How can he stand to comprehend the hard, pitiful
Unrelenting cycles of coitus, ovipositors, sperm and
    zygotes,
The repeated unions and dissolutions over and over,

The constant tenacious burying and covering and
        hiding
And nesting, the furious nurturing of eggs, the bright
Breaking-forth and the inevitable cold blowing-away?
Think of the million million dried stems of decaying
Dragonflies, the thousand thousand leathery cavities
Of old toads, the mounds of cows' teeth, the tufts
Of torn fur, the contorted eyes, the broken feet, the rank
Bloated odors, the fecund brown-haired mildews
That are the residue of his process. How can he tolerate
        knowing
There is nothing else here on earth as bright and salty
As blood spilled in the open?

Maybe he wakes periodically at night,
Wiping away the tears he doesn't know
He has cried in his sleep, not having had time yet to tell
Himself precisely how it is he must mourn, not having
        had time yet
To elicit from his creation its invention
Of his own solace.

Inside God's Eye

As if his eye had no boundaries, at night
All the heavens are visible there. The stars drift
And hesitate inside that sphere like white seeds
Sinking in a still, dark lake. Spirals of brilliance,
They float silently and slowly deeper and deeper
Into the possible expansion of his acuity.
And within that watching, illumination like the moon
Is uncovered petal by petal as a passing cloud clears
The open white flowers of the shining summer plum.

Inside god's eye, light spreads as afternoon spreads,

Accepting the complications of water burr and
     chestnut,
The efforts of digger bee and cuckoo bee. Even the
     barest
Light gathers and concentrates there like a ray
Of morning reaching the thinnest nerve of a fairy
     shrimp
At the center of a pond. And like evening, light
Bends inside the walls of god's eye to make
Skywide globes of fuchsia and orange, violet-tipped
Branches and violet-tinged wings set against a red dusk.

Lines from the tangle of dodder, bindweed
And honeysuckle, from the interweaving knot
Of seaweed and cones, patterns from the network
Of blowing shadow and flashing poplar, fill
And define the inner surface moment of his retina.

And we, we are the only point of reversal
Inside his eye, the only point of light
That turns back on itself and by that turning
Saves time from infinity and saves motion
From obscurity. We are the vessel and the blood
And the pulse he sees as he sees the eye watching
The vision inside his eye in the perfect mirror
Held constantly before his face.

Before the Beginning: Maybe God and a
Silk Flower Concubine Perhaps

The white sky is exactly the same white
stone as the white marble of the transparent
earth, and the moon with its clear white
swallow makes of its belly of rock neither
absence nor presence.

The stars are not syllables yet enunciated
by his potential white tongue, its vestigial
lick a line that might break eventually,
a horizon curving enough to pronounce
at last, *my love.*

The locked and frigid porcelain barrens
and hollows of the descending black plain
are a pattern of gardens only to any single
blind eye blinking, just as a possible stroke
of worm, deaf with whiteness, might hear
a lace bud of silk meridians spinning
and unraveling simultaneously on the vacuous
beds of the placeless firmament.

An atheist might believe in the seductive
motion turning beneath the transparent gown
covering invisibly the non-existent bones
and petals of no other. Thus the holy blossom,
spread like the snow impression of a missing
angel, doubts the deep-looped vacancy
of her own being into which god, in creation,
must assuredly come.

Is it possible there might be silver seeds
placed deep between those legs opening
like a parting of fog to reveal the plunging salt
of a frothy sea? But god digresses, dreaming
himself a ghost, with neither clamor nor ecstasy,
into inertia, his name being farther
than ever from time.

Static on the unendurably boring white
sheet of his own plane, he must think hard
toward that focus of conception when he can rise

shuddering, descending and erupting into the beauty
and fragrance of their own making together—
those flowering orange-scarlet layers and sun-
shocking blue heavens of, suddenly, one another.

In Addition to Faith, Hope and Charity

I'm sure there's a god
in favor of drums. Consider
their pervasiveness—the thump,
thump and slide of waves
on a stretched hide of beach,
the rising beat and slap
of their crests against shore
baffles, the rapping of otters
cracking molluscs with stones,
woodpeckers beak-banging, the beaver's
whack of his tail-paddle, the ape
playing the bam of his own chest,
the million tickering rolls
of rain off the flat-leaves
and razor-rims of the forest.

And we know the noise
of our own inventions—snare and kettle,
bongo, conga, big bass, toy tin,
timbals, tambourine, tom-tom.

But the heart must be the most
pervasive drum of all. Imagine
hearing all together every tinny
snare of every heartbeat
in every jumping mouse and harvest
mouse, sagebrush vole and least

shrew living across the prairie;
and add to that cacophony the individual
staccato tickings inside all gnatcatchers,
kingbirds, kestrels, rock doves, pine
warblers crossing, criss-crossing
each other in the sky, the sound
of their beatings overlapping
with the singular hammerings
of the hearts of cougar, coyote,
weasel, badger, pronghorn, the ponderous
bass of the black bear; and on deserts too,
all the knackings, the flutterings
inside wart snakes, whiptails, racers
and sidewinders, earless lizards, cactus
owls; plus the clamors undersea, slow
booming in the breasts of beluga
and bowhead, uniform rappings
in a passing school of cod or bib,
the thidderings of bat rays and needlefish.

Imagine the earth carrying this continuous
din, this multifarious festival of pulsing
thuds, stutters and drummings, wheeling
on and on across the universe.

This must be proof of a power existing
somewhere definitely in favor
of such a racket.

For the Future Evolution of the God of the Abyss

You who endures the repetitious
whipcrack and futile speed everywhere
stizzling in hapless, faltering

orbits, god of the hollow
at the core of the blasphemy
of the before and the blasphemy

of the final, being of and within
that void where sight cannot follow
and echo never returns, who is best

beheld in the unimagined
cavities of nameless oblivions
and temples of emptiness, who is

the never in all rantings
of extinction spat and stuttered
about like pieces of burnt newspaper

gusted down a winter street, the god
who is wrapped and bound and formed
by the question never formed,

the flame after the candle
is placed upside down in the dish,
you who bears your own vacuity

and your own nonentity, who retains
the essence of loss like a comet
in cycle bears and becomes the dust

of its own disintegration—within
the vast null and lack composing
your missing, remember us

made in your image, and then be
our pity, and then be our hope.

"God Is In The Details," Says Mathematician
Freeman J. Dyson

This is why grandmother takes such tiny
stitches, one stitch for each dust mote
of moon on the Serengeti at night, and one half
one stitch for each salt-fetch of fog
following the geometries of eelgrasses
in fields along the beach.

And this is why she changes the brief threads
in her glass needle so often—metallic bronze
for the halo around the thrasher's eye,
ruby diaphanous for the antenna tips
of the May beetle, transparent silk
for dry-rain fragrances blowing
through bur sages before rain.

She inserts her needle
through the center of each elementary
particle, as if it were a circling sequin
of blue, loops it to its orbit, sewing thus,
again and again, the reckless sapphire sea,
a whipping flag of tall summer sky.

Sometimes she takes in her hands
two slight breaths of needles at once,
needles so thin they almost burn
her fingers like splinters of light.
She crochets with them around each microscopic
void, invents, thereby, an ice tapestry
of winter on the window, creates a lace
of peeper shrillings through flooded
sweet gale, secures a blank jot of sight
in the knitting of each red flea
of zooplankton skittering mid-lake.

God's most minute exuberance is founded
in the way she sews with needles
as assertive as the sun-sharp loblolly
that she sees with her eyes closed;
in the way she knots stitches
as interlocked as the cries of veery,
peewee, black-capped chickadee and jay
that she hears with her ears stopped;
in the way she whispers to her work,
recites to her work, spooling every least
designation of spicule shade, hay
spider and air trifid, every hue
and rising act of her own hands. *Try
to escape now,* it reads, *just try.*

Pattiann Rogers

A PORTRAIT

by Scott Slovic

Picture Pattiann Rogers picturing herself picturing the world, with her eyes closed and her mind wide open. A little girl, four or five years old, imagines that she will never know how she looks to the rest of the world when her eyes are closed; her mother, free spirited and generous, photographs her daughter on a backyard stoop, eyes closed, smiling. Remembering this scene years later, the poet explains in her essay, "The Dream of the Marsh Wren," "This was my way, at the time, of wondering about self and existence, about perception and perception of self and concept of self." Today Pattiann Rogers continues this process of exploration with the same smiling wonderment her mother facilitated in the 1940s in small-town Missouri. Her poetry, collected in eight volumes so far, likewise gently facilitates her own readers' personal and cosmic meditations, teasing out a capacity for mystery among even the most hardened, rational thinkers among us.

I recall the first time I ever heard her address a group. There were twenty of us gathered in March 1996 at Ann Zwinger's mountain home, Constant Friendship, located in the Rockies west of Colorado Springs, to celebrate Ann's acceptance of the Orion Society's John Hay Award for lifetime achievement in the field of natural history writing. On Sunday morning, the final day of our weekend of celebration and discussion, Pattiann sat on the sunny wooden porch of the Zwingers' house, not far from Ann's famous aspen grove, reflecting on nature and the sacred for a ragtag audience of friends—scholars and editors and fellow writers—including Gary Paul Nabhan, Robert Michael Pyle, and Kim Stafford. I can remember only fragments of Pattiann's remarks (published later that year as the essay "What Among Heavens and Suns," *Orion Society Notebook*), read from notes in blue ink on a yellow legal pad, but what I did carry away with me was the strong feeling of reassurance—it's okay to wonder, it's okay to acknowledge the mysterious workings of the world, it's okay to seek a language for registering this sense of the unknown. It's okay and even delightful to explore and to share one's findings with a community of readers and listeners. Something about Pattiann Rogers's very demeanor, her neat-but-not-fussy hair that, propped up by her glasses, hangs over her ears and nearly across her eyes, her informal style of dress (often slacks and tennis shoes), her ready smile and soft twangy voice—something about this woman says, whether she's writing or speaking, "It's okay to have fun with your mind, to think deep thoughts about the world, about yourself."

When I read the essay's opening poem, "The Dream of the Marsh Wren: Reciprocal Creation," I found myself thinking of something the poet told Richard McCann back in 1985 in an interview later published in *The Iowa Review:* "The poetry has created me at the same time that I was creating the poetry. . . ." Likewise, this book of exploration and explanation, her first book of prose, offers herself and her readers a rich realm of supposition and speculation, a realm of "reciprocal creation." This is one of Pattiann Rogers's major gifts: the gift not only of her own playful, profound meditations, but the gift of the *process* of playful, profound meditation to her audience.

Read the poem "Suppose Your Father Was a Redbird" toward the beginning of her essay, and substitute a few new words. It's okay, it's part of the process. Suppose your mother was a poet. How would this affect your vision of yourself and the world? Worldview, perspective, the workings of the individual mind, the similarities and differences among species—all of these ideas are probed in this particular poem and in many of Rogers's poems of supposition. And although we do not all have mothers quite like her, we can learn about the "reciprocal creation" between the poet-mother and her inquisitive children by reading her personal narratives of motherhood and art. The poems themselves are like the gifts of insight and perspective a mother might offer her friends and her children.

Given her proclivity to suppose wild things about the universe, Rogers runs the constant risk of her ideas evaporating into abstract discourse. She runs this risk, but has little to fear, for the counterpart to her love of speculation is her fascination with the physical world. In her interview with McCann, when asked how she would write a poem if she were transported to a new space station, she replied:

> The way I would begin a poem like that would be the way I would begin any poem. I would start with the senses, and I would start with my sensual pleasure in what I was experiencing; or I would describe a physical object very carefully and then see if anything else rose out of that. That to me is the salvation. Salvation is in the physical object, whether it's my body, a locust, an egret, an iris, or a man-made object in space. In the particular object lies all that I discover.

Rogers's *Credo* essay anchors the intense lyricism of her poetry in the lived experiences that generated her work, contextualizing and making even more concrete her already physical poetry. What gave her the idea to write such famous poems as "Justification of the Horned Lizard" and "The Importance of the Whale in the Field of Iris" and "Rolling Naked in the Morning Dew" and "The Family Is All There Is"? Where did these poems come from? What were her thought processes during the writing? With extraordinary candor, and with the self-deprecating humor well known to all who have heard her perform, the poet reflects upon these questions.

Pattiann Rogers was born on March 23, 1940, in Joplin, Missouri. Her mother, Irene Keiter Tall, had a junior college education and worked as an elementary school teacher until her marriage to Pattiann's father, William Elmer Tall. Her parents had planned to be married in Kansas City, Missouri, but because it was against the law at that time for school teachers in Missouri to marry, her parents had to get in a taxi with the minister and travel across the state line into Kansas for their wedding. "So they were married in a taxi," the poet reports with impish delight (personal correspondence).

Pattiann's brother, William E. Tall, Jr., was born four and a half years before her. Irene Tall worked as a homemaker while her children were young, and was active in the Presbyterian Church and as a volunteer for various civic organizations. She was also a gardener and a seamstress, an excellent cook, and an industrious canner of most of the fruits and vegetables that her family ate. In 1952, when Pattiann was in junior high school, her mother helped to establish George Washington Carver Memorial Nursery School in Joplin, years before the development of government-sponsored preschool programs for children of working parents. The nonprofit school, still in operation today, was founded by Mrs. Martha Cuther, an African

American woman. Enrollment in the school was 98 percent African American, and Irene Tall served as director for seventeen years, working with a staff composed of both caucasians and African Americans. Pattiann worked there in the afternoons of her junior and senior years of high school. "I remember once holding a small, four-year-old boy named Kenny on my lap during afternoon nap time," she writes. "He had a smallpox vaccination that was painful, and he was fretful. This was the first time I realized that my presence could bring comfort to someone else. I've never forgotten the joy of discovering that" (personal correspondence).

William Tall had only an eighth-grade education. A native Canadian, he never became a U.S. citizen and had to register each year as a resident alien. His mother died of tuberculosis when he was two years old, and his father remarried and had seven children with his second wife. William ran away from home when he was fourteen. He had many different jobs during his life, owning a tire company for a while and later an appliance store, which burned down on Pattiann's tenth birthday. Energetic, fun-loving, and imaginative, he helped to mold some of the most important aspects of his children's intellectual lives. Like Pattiann, her brother William leaned toward the arts; he played four musical instruments as a boy and went on to become a visual artist, even creating the artwork for the covers of her books *The Tattooed Lady in the Garden* and *Splitting and Binding*. But the family's economic situation was erratic. As Pattiann recalls, "sometimes we had plenty of money, but there were many times of scarcity" (personal correspondence).

Pattiann met her husband, John Robert Rogers, also a native Missourian, when they were both undergraduates at the University of Missouri in Columbia. They met in French class, where they were the top two students in the class. They were married in 1960, and Pattiann completed her degree in English literature a year later. While John worked on his Ph.D. in physics at the University of Missouri in Rolla, Pattiann supported them by working as a kindergarten teacher in nearby St. James. Their first son, John Ashley, was born August 24, 1967, in Rolla; Arthur William followed three years later on August 22, by which time the family had moved to Houston, Texas, so that John Rogers could do geophysical research for Texaco and pursue postgraduate training in geology at the University of Houston.

Like her own mother, Pattiann devoted herself to her children during their early years. As the *Credo* essay demonstrates, her children taught her important things about looking at the world, opening up the mind and heart to the world: "reciprocal creation." She continues to be intrigued by the scientific sensibility of her son John and her husband; regarding the latter, she writes, "His mind works in a way different from mine and yet complementary in a strange way. He generally has a perspective that's surprising to me and information that I find fascinating" (personal correspondence). Her son earned a Ph.D. in physics at MIT in 1995, was a Junior Fellow at Harvard, and now runs a physics lab at Bell Labs; his wife, also an MIT Ph.D., has her own lab in the chemistry department at Bell Labs. These close family connections with the scientific world help to explain Pattiann's readiness to embrace concepts and vocabulary from the physical sciences in her artistic work. In a 1997 interview with Casey Walker for the *Wild Duck Review,* she stated:

> Now, I love science. I live with a scientist. One of my sons and my daughter-in-law are scientists. Even before we were married, my husband, John, would tell me the history of physics as if it were a grand story. Scientists were adventurers who were going into the unknown. Yet, although I love science, the process of science not just its results, it's never going to totally explain the human experience. And I think scientists will be the first to admit that, most of them anyway. . . . Certainly the vocabularies of science have been rich sources for my work. But science alone can hardly fulfill our spiritual needs. One of the aims of my writing that I was able to explain to myself early was that I wanted to try to express some of the things I found exciting and exhilarating about what science was doing, but, at the same time, to ask how we might incorporate the cosmology of science into our need for a spiritual life.

If the physical sciences can tell us only so much about our inner lives, then some of the answers about the human mind can be explored through literature and through such sciences as psychology. Arthur, her younger son, shares this inclination and earned his degrees in English and psychology at the University of Texas at Austin. He now makes his living creating and developing on-line, interactive computer games.

While Pattiann and her family were living in Houston, she enrolled in the new graduate program in creative writing at the University of Houston, eventually becoming the program's first graduate when she completed her M.A. in 1981. That same year, Princeton University Press published her first book of poetry, *The Expectations of Light,* which received the Texas Institute of Letters Award for poetry and inspired reviewer Peter Stitt to notice her "sophisticated incorporation of modern scientific thinking into poetry." Her second poetry collection, *The Tattooed Lady in the Garden,* published by Wesleyan University Press in 1986, extends her scientific reflections into the psychological dimension, citing Werner Heisenberg's famous claim that "what we observe is not nature itself but nature exposed to our method of questioning." A number of the poems in this collection, from "A Daydream of Light" to "The Possible Suffering of a God During Creation"

and "Justification of the Horned Lizard," explore *how* we know things about the world and how nonhuman minds respond to existence. Her trademark "poetry of supposition" also begins to emerge prominently in this collection. Rogers taught as a visiting professor at Southern Methodist University, the University of

Houston, the University of Texas–Austin, and Vermont College between 1985 and 1989, and served as the Richard Hugo Distinguished Poet-in-Residence at the University of Montana for the spring term of 1988. Although she and her husband John live in Castle Rock, Colorado, she has spent most spring semesters since 1993 teaching at the University of Arkansas, where she is an associate professor, plus a stint as visiting professor at Washington University in St. Louis in fall 1995. Her many awards include several prizes from *Poetry Northwest* and *Poetry* in the early 1980s, National Endowment for the Arts Grants in 1982 and 1988, and a Guggenheim Fellowship in 1984–85. Ion Press published *Legendary Performance* in 1987 and Wesleyan published *Splitting and Binding* in 1989.

It was *Splitting and Binding* that seems to have solidified her reputation as an American poet of the first rank. As Marsha Engelbrecht writes for the *Dictionary of Literary Biography,* Rogers's emphasis in this book

> is on the reverent witnessing and praising of all aspects of the natural world. Through her unwavering gaze, readers experience startling images that strike a wide range of sensory chords. Rogers presents many sights and sounds, including eerie phosphorescent creatures of the ocean depths, shrieking blue jays in grief, and hissing geese protecting their nests. Interspersed throughout the book are poems that are pure celebration of physical

sensation. This format is one of Rogers's specialties.

A year after this book appeared, she received the Soerette Diehl Fraser/Natalie Ornish Poetry Award from the Texas Institute of Letters, followed by the Strousse Award from *Prairie Schooner* and a poetry fellowship from the Lannan Foundation in 1992.

The steady stream of poetry collections continued with *Geocentric* appearing from Gibbs Smith in 1993 and *Firekeeper: New and Selected Poems* in 1994. In the wake of *Firekeeper,* Rogers was described as a priestess, a physicist, a natural theologian, and an erotic poet—all of these epithets describe parts of her accomplishment in this major book, which was chosen by *Publishers Weekly* as one of the best books published that year and was a finalist for the Lenore Marshall Award from the Academy of American Poets. The work was further honored by a third poetry award from the Texas Institute of Letters. Reviewing *Firekeeper* for *Poetry,* Leslie Ullman offers some of the most prescient comments on her work:

> These poems are consistently sensuous in their savorings and inventions, their probings, and their continual delight not only in all forms of life but also in the fecundity of language. Even as they draw the reader into a mating dance or seed-hatching by choreographing it on the page, or describe a parlor so that we can almost see the color of air amid the brocade cushions and the smoke of

slender cigarettes, Rogers's poems also aban-
don themselves to the singular tastes and
shapes of words.

In 1997, Milkweed Editions, publisher of *Fire-
keeper*, produced *Eating Bread and Honey*, which not
only continues Rogers's kaleidoscopic meditations on
the emotional and physical implications of divinity,
but offers one of the most ethically challenging
poems about the relationship between humans and
animals ever written. Toward the end of "Animals and
People: 'The Human Heart in Conflict with Itself',"
she writes:

> We know we are one with them,
> and we are frantic to understand how to actualize that
>   union.
> We attempt to actualize that union in our many
>   stumbling,
> ignorant and destructive ways, in our many confused
> and noble and praiseworthy ways.
>
> For how can we possess dignity
> if we allow them no dignity? Who will recognize our
>   beauty
> if we do not revel in their beauty? How can we hope
> to receive honor if we give no honor? How can we
>   believe
> in grace if we cannot bestow grace?

If there has been a shift in Rogers's more recent work,
perhaps it is evident in the increasingly daring vigor
of her merging science and spirituality, perhaps in

the more direct articulation of social consciousness, as is demonstrated in the poem above. An example of the daring, almost taunting, linkage of body and spirit appears in the poem "The Fallacy of Thinking Flesh Is Flesh," which concludes, "Even as it sleeps, watch the body / perplex its definition—the slight shift / of the spine, the inevitable lash shiver, / signal pulse knocking. See, there, / that simple shimmer of the smallest / toe again, just to prove it." As Ullman puts it in her earlier review of *Firekeeper,* "While Rogers's vision is firmly rooted in nature, it would be reductive to call her a nature poet; her poems are gestures of a spirit that experiences the act of observation as religious, a ritual as vital as eating or drawing breath."

The year 1998 saw the publication of Pattiann Rogers's eighth book, *A Covenant of Seasons,* prepared in collaboration with the artist Joellyn Duesberry, and her continued offering of numerous public readings. Rogers has given more than 150 public readings since 1981; her willingness to perform has, like so many other aspects of her life, become part of the "reciprocal creation" in her work. Her poems are written to match the cadences of her speech, and the stories of her life are coextensive with the contexts of her verse. As she travels around the country sharing new poems and old favorites, such as "Rolling Naked in the Morning Dew" and "The Hummingbird: A Seduction," she responds to crowds like a troubadour, taking requests and bantering with her listeners. At a recent conference, a professor called out his request for "The Hummingbird," and she laughed back, "Ah, you're the one who has to ask his students to throw water on him after discussing that poem in class, aren't you?"

Sensuality and spirituality, raw wonderment and antic comedy—these are some of the key dimensions of Pattiann Rogers's extraordinary poetry. And these are the form and content of her *Credo* essay as well.

Bibliography of Pattiann Rogers's Work

by Scott Slovic

BOOKS

With Joellyn Duesberry. *A Covenant of Seasons.* New York: Hudson Hill Press, 1998.

Eating Bread and Honey. Minneapolis: Milkweed Editions, 1997.

Firekeeper: New and Selected Poems. Minneapolis: Milkweed Editions, 1994.

Geocentric. Salt Lake City: Gibbs Smith, 1993.

Splitting and Binding. Middletown, Conn.: Wesleyan University Press, 1989.

Legendary Performance. Memphis: Ion Press, 1987.

The Tattooed Lady in the Garden. Middletown, Conn.: Wesleyan University Press, 1986.

The Expectations of Light. Princeton: Princeton University Press, 1981.

CHAPBOOKS

Lies and Devotions. Berkeley: Tangram Press, 1994.

The Only Holy Window. Denton, Tex.: Trilobite Press, 1984.

The Ark River Review: Three Poet Issue. Wichita: Ark River Review, 1981.

UNCOLLECTED JOURNAL AND MAGAZINE PUBLICATIONS—POEMS

"Almanac." *The Hudson Review* (forthcoming).

"The Stars Beneath My Feet" and "The Making of the World." *The Iowa Review* (forthcoming).

"Ting, Ting," "God's Sabbath," and "Around Each and Every." *Midwest Quarterly* (forthcoming).

"Born of a Rib" and "The Blessings of Ashes and Dust." *Orion* (forthcoming).

"Archetype." *The Paris Review* (forthcoming).

"Facility and Distinction" and "The Known Unknown." *Prairie Schooner* (forthcoming).

"Old Woman and a Tramp." *Seattle Review* (forthcoming).

"Speaking of Evolution: Luminosity," "Being the Love of the Insane," "The Puzzle of Serenity," and "Disunion: Moonless Hound Monologue." *Washington Square* (forthcoming).

"The Nature of the Huckster." *Wilderness* (forthcoming).

"As the Living Are to the Dead" and "Silva." *Cortland Review* (www.cortlandreview.com), no. 7 (May 1999).

"Body and Soul and the Other," "This Love, Within and Without a Moment's Thought," and "Stranger." *The Tampa Review* (Spring 1999): 30–32.

"Being Specific," "Suitor," and "This Salvation."
Alkali Flats, no. 1 (Fall 1998): 15–18.

"Jacob's Ladder." *Boston College Magazine* 58, no. 4
(Fall 1998): 13.

"Watching the Ancestral Prayers of Venerable
Others." *DoubleTake* 4, no. 4 (Fall 1998): 109.

"elegance" and "Motion in Philosophy." *River City*
18 and 19, nos. 2 and 1 (Summer 1998): 82–85.

"On the Way to Early Morning Mass" and "Reitera-
tion." *Poetry* 171, no. 3 (January 1998): 198–201.

"The Lexicographer's Prayer," ". . . the indivisible
universe . . . ," and "The Bearers of Flowers." *Notre
Dame Review,* no. 5. (Winter 1998): 31–37.

"Peace All Seasons, Each Night." *Western Humanities
Review* 52, no. 4 (Winter 1998): 294–95.

"The Composer, The Bone Yard." *The Paris Review,*
no. 143 (Summer 1997): 224–25.

"Come, Drink Here." *The Hudson Review* 50, no. 1
(Spring 1997): 98–99.

"Moon Deer, the Vision of Their Making" and "He
Who Greets with Fire." *Interdisciplinary Studies in
Literature and Environment* 4, no. 1 (Spring 1997):
121–22, 124–25.

"Afterward" and "Gospel." *The Gettysburg Review* 10,
no. 4 (Winter 1997): 568–70.

"The Metal Lion and the Monk" and "Variations on
Breaking the Faith of Sleep." *Gulf Coast Review* 9,
no. 1 (Winter 1997): 42–44.

"Fossil Texts on Canyon Walls" and "The Defining
Point." *Weber Studies* 14, no. 1 (Winter 1997):
134–36.

"these horses never cease." *Poetry International,* no. 1 (1997): 94–95.

"Easter Frogs." *Seattle Review* 19, no. 1 (1997): 43–44.

"Parallel Universes." *Poetry Northwest* 37, no. 1 (Spring 1996): 43–44.

"The Form of That Which Is Sought" and "Caressing Creatures." *New Letters* 62, no. 4 (1996): 28–31.

"Being Known: Goldfinches at Sea" and "The China Cabinet Festival: Twenty-First Century." *Crab Orchard Review* 1, no. 1 (Fall/Winter 1995): 93–96.

"Calling to Measure." *Poetry* 166, no. 2 (May 1995): 97–98.

"Shrine," "Dust Birds: The Will of a Landscape to Be Eternal," and "Believing in Blood." *Fine Madness* 21 (1995): 2, 4–7.

"Idée Fixe" and "Sensual Deprivation." *Weber Studies* 11, no. 3 (Fall 1994): 30–32.

*"A New Notice of Motion: The Lover Waiting," "Death Vision," and *"Considering All the Moving Light, All the Stationary Darkness." *Kenyon Review* 15, no. 4 (Fall 1993): 128–31.

"Truth as We Know It." *Michigan Quarterly Review* 32, no. 3 (Summer 1993): 352–53.

"The One True God." *Cutbank* 39 (Winter 1993): 3–4.

"Crux," "Winter Camping," and "Life History and the Plain Facts." *South Carolina Review* 25, no. 1 (Fall 1992): 12–15.

"Prism, Art and Craft." *Fine Madness* 9, no. 1 (Spring/Summer 1992): 6.

*"Rocking and Resurrection." *Indiana Review* 15, no. 1 (Spring 1992): 56–57.

"The Insight of Limitations" and "Seeing Cat Things,

Human Things, God Things." *New England Review* 13, nos. 3/4 (Spring/Summer 1991): 293–94.

*"God's Only Begotten Daughter" and *"Abomination." *Poetry Northwest* 32, no. 1 (Spring 1991): 4–5, 6–7.

"Her Repast," "The Older Kid," and "Faith and Certainty: Arctic Circles." *Prairie Schooner* 65, no. 1 (Spring 1991): 19, 20, 22–24.

*"The Seeming of Things" and "Prairie Garden, Midnight, Moonless." *Western Humanities Review* 45, no. 4 (Winter 1991): 300–301, 303.

"Seeing the God-Statement" and "More Recollection." *Missouri Review* 13, no. 3 (1991): 90–93.

"An Assumption," "The Shape and Weight of Belief," and "Sea Saviors." *Indiana Review* 13, no. 3 (Fall 1990): 1–7.

*"The Blind Beggar's Dog," *Crazyhorse* 38 (Spring 1990): 16–17.

"Next to Sleep" and "Grandmother's Sister." *River City* 10, no. 1 (Fall 1989): 1–3.

*"In an Open Field on a Clear Night," "Earth-Night Errors," and "The God of Sunday Evening, June 7, 1987." *Poetry Northwest* 30, no. 2 (Summer 1989): 4–7.

"Repeat and Repeat" and "The Fear of Non-Being." *Laurel Review* 23, no. 2 (Summer 1989): 45–47.

"The Woodland Snail at Twilight." *Fine Madness* 5, no. 2 (Fall 1988): 62–63.

"Predestination." *TriQuarterly* 73 (Fall 1988): 129–30.

"Playroom: The Visionaries" and "The Message." *Cream City Review* 12, no. 2 (Summer 1988): 255–56, 259.

"Capturing a Wild Pony." *Fine Madness* 5, no. 1 (Spring 1988): 4–5.

"How the Old See Death." *Poetry* 151, no. 4 (January 1988): 357–58.

"Beyond All Ken." *Cutbank* 31/32 (1988): 42–43.

"Taking Leave." *Missouri Review* 11, no. 1 (1988): 14–15.

"Nothing Moves Like the Moon." *Gulf Coast Review* 2, no. 1 (Fall/Winter 1987–88): 34.

"Pity My Simplicity." *Prairie Schooner* 60, no. 4 (Winter 1986): 80–81.

"The Way of Creation." *Black Warrior Review* 12, no. 2 (Spring 1986): 27–28.

"The Thing in Itself." *Poetry* 147, no. 4 (January 1986): 215–16.

"Coming Back." *Poetry Northwest* 26, no. 2 (Summer 1985): 29–30.

"Variations on a Symbol," "With His Own Two Eyes," and "The Insight of the Pentastich." *Chowder Review,* nos. 20–21 (Summer 1985): 71–72, 75–78.

"Variations on a Vision." *Seattle Review* 8, no. 1 (Spring 1985): 15–16.

"The Creation of Protest." *Virginia Quarterly* 61, no. 1 (Winter 1985): 60–61.

"The Elegance of the Dichotomous Experience." *Poetry* 144, no. 6 (September 1984): 341.

"Creating Something Out of Nothing" and "Rhythmic Brushwork." *Kenyon Review* 6, no. 2 (Spring 1984): 60–62.

"Stripes of the Sea: Multiple Images and the Spaces Between." *Crazyhorse* 26 (Spring 1984): 49.

"The Art of Imitation." *Missouri Review* 7, no. 3 (1984): 29.

"Cecil Paints the Gypsy of a Thousand Veils Dancing on the Prairie at Dawn" and "Making Pure Spirit Perfect." *Sonora Review* 7 (1984): 83–86.

*"The Body is Filled with Light" and *"The Place of Juxtaposition." *Poetry Northwest* 24, no. 4 (Winter 1983–84): 22–23.

"Statement Preliminary to the Invention of Solace" and *"The Body as Window." *Poetry* 143, no. 1 (October 1983): 3–6.

"I Thought I Heard a White-Haired Man with a Purple Tie Say, 'The Mind Creates What It Perceives'." *Massachusetts Review* 24, no. 4 (Winter 1983): 719–20.

"Keeping the Body Warm." *Massachusetts Review* 23, no. 4 (Winter 1982): 555–56.

"Being What We Are," and "Finding the Cat in a Spring Field at Midnight." *Poetry* 141, no. 3 (December 1982): 132, 134–35.

*"Light of the Sea," "The Revolution of the Dream," "The Imagination Imagines Itself to be God," and *"To Burn Forever." *Poetry Northwest* 23, no. 3 (Autumn 1982): 10–15.

"The Abandonment." *Poetry* 140, no. 1 (April 1982): 32–33.

"Pursuing the Study of a Particular Reality" and "Rumors of Snow, Christmas Eve." *Poetry Northwest* (Spring 1982): 38–39, 40–41.

"The Boredom of the Isolated." *Chicago Review* 33, no. 2 (1982): 123.

"Mastering the Calm." *Poetry Northwest* 22, no. 3
(Autumn 1981): 7–8.
*"The Last Blessing." *Poetry* 137, no. 1 (April 1981):
30.

Poems contained in limited-edition chapbooks.

UNCOLLECTED JOURNAL AND MAGAZINE
PUBLICATIONS—ESSAYS

"The Evocation of Rain." *Portland Magazine* (Autumn
1998).
"Keeping Love's Promise." *U.S. Catholic* (May 1998).
"Surprised by the Sacred." *U.S. Catholic* (March
1998).
". . . for me mothers, and the mothers of moth-
ers . . ." *Portland Magazine* (Spring 1997).
"What Among Heavens and Suns." *Orion Society
Notebook* (Winter 1996).
"Cradle." *Orion* (Fall 1995).
"Thoreau and Mothers." *Northern Lights* (Summer
1992).

ANTHOLOGY APPEARANCES

The Best Spiritual Writing, 1999, edited by Philip
Zaleski. San Francisco: HarperSanFrancisco,
forthcoming.
*And What Rough Beast, Poems at the End of the
Century,* edited by Robert McGovern and Stephen
Haven. Ashland, Ohio: Ashland Poetry Press,
1999.
From Sight to Insight: Stages in the Writing Process, ed-
ited by Jeff Rackham and Olivia Bertagnolli.

1987. Sixth edition by New York: Holt, Rinehart and Winston, 1999.

Literature: Timeless Voices, Timeless Themes. Upper Saddle River, N.J.: Prentice Hall, 1999.

Literature and the Environment, edited by Lorraine Anderson, Scott Slovic, and John P. O'Grady. New York: Addison Wesley Longman, 1999.

Best Texas Writing, edited by Joe Ahearn and Brian Clements. Dallas: Rancho Loco Press, 1998.

The Book of Love, edited by Diane Ackerman and Jeanne Mackin. New York: Norton, 1998.

Intimate Nature: The Bond between Women and Animals, edited by Linda Hogan, Deena Metzger, and Brenda Peterson. New York: Ballantine, 1998.

Pillow: Exploring the Heart of Eros, edited by Lily Pond. Berkeley: A Yellow Silk Book, 1998.

Pushcart Prize Twenty-Three: Best of the Small Presses, edited by Bill Henderson. Wainscott, N.Y.: Pushcart Press, 1998.

Verse and Universe: Poems about Science and Mathematics, edited by Kurt Brown. Minneapolis: Milkweed Editions, 1998.

Wild Song: Poems of the Natural World, edited by John Daniel. Athens: University of Georgia Press, 1998.

Poetry: Eighty-Fifth Anniversary Issue, edited by Joseph Parisi. Chicago: Modern Poetry Association, 1997.

The Portable Western Reader, edited by William Kittredge. New York: Penguin, 1997.

The Best American Poetry 1996, selected by Adrienne Rich, edited by David Lehman. New York: Scribner, 1996.

Chicago Review: Fifty Years: A Retrospective Issue, edited by David Nicholls. Chicago: University of Chicago Press, 1996.

Claiming the Spirit Within, edited by Marilyn Sewell. Boston: Beacon Press, 1996.

Hard Choices: An Iowa Reader, edited by David Hamilton. Iowa City: University of Iowa Press, 1996.

A Forest of Voices, edited by Chris Anderson and Lex Runciman. Mountain View, Calif.: Mayfield, 1995.

From the Island's Edge: A Sitka Reader, edited by Carolyn Servid. St. Paul: Graywolf Press, 1995.

High Fantastic, edited by Steve Rasnic Tem. Denver: Ocean View Books, 1995.

Poems for the Wild Earth, edited by Gary Lawless. Nobleboro, Maine: Blackberry Books, 1995.

The Poetry Dictionary, edited by John Drury. Cincinnati: Story Press, 1995.

What Will Suffice: Contemporary Poets on the Art of Poetry, edited by Christopher Buckley and Christopher Merrill. Salt Lake City: Gibbs Smith Publisher, 1995.

Writing It Down for James: Writers on Craft and Life, edited by Kurt Brown. Boston: Beacon Press, 1995.

The Writing Path One: Poetry and Prose from Writers' Conferences, edited by Michael Pettit. Iowa City: University of Iowa Press, 1995.

Articulations, edited by Jon Mukand. Iowa City: University of Iowa Press, 1994.

Texas in Poetry: A 150 Year Anthology, edited by Billy Bob Hill. Denton: Center for Texas Studies, University of North Texas, 1994.

The Wesleyan Tradition: Four Decades of American Poetry, edited by Michael Collier. Middletown: Wesleyan University Press, 1994.

Women on Hunting, edited by Pam Houston. Hopewell, N.J.: Ecco Press, 1994.

Poetry, edited by R. S. Gwynn. New York: HarperCollins, 1993.

The Sophisticated Cat, edited by Joyce Carol Oates. New York: Dutton, 1993.

Where We Stand: Women Poets on the Literary Tradition, edited by Sharon Bryan. New York: Norton, 1993.

Pushcart Prize Seventeen: Best of the Small Presses, edited by Bill Henderson. Wainscott, N.Y.: Avon, 1992.

American Poets of the Nineties, edited by Jack Myers and Roger Weingarten. Boston: David R. Godine, 1991.

The Forgotten Language: Contemporary Poets and Nature, edited by Christopher Merrill. Salt Lake City: Gibbs Smith, 1991.

Heart of the Flower: Poems for the Sensuous Gardener, edited by Sondra Zeidenstein. Goshen, Conn.: Chicory Blue Press, 1991.

The Norton Introduction to Literature, edited by Carl E. Bain, Jerome Beaty, and J. Paul Hunter. 5th ed. New York: Norton, 1991.

The Norton Introduction to Poetry, edited by J. Paul Hunter. 4th ed. New York: Norton, 1991.

Sisters of the Earth, edited by Lorraine Anderson. New York: Vintage, 1991.

Introduction to Poetry, edited by James Pickering

and Jeffrey Hoeper. New York: Macmillan,
1990.

Looking for Home: Women Writing about Exile, edited
by Deborah Keenan and Roseann Lloyd.
Minneapolis: Milkweed Editions, 1990.

*Vital Signs: Contemporary American Poetry from the
University Presses,* edited by Ronald Wallace.
Madison: University of Wisconsin Press, 1990.

Literature: The Power of Language, edited by Thomas
McLaughlin. Orlando, Fla.: Harcourt Brace
Jovanovich, 1989.

Pushcart Prize Fourteen: Best of the Small Presses, edited
by Bill Henderson. Wainscott, N.Y.: Avon, 1989.

The Discovery of Poetry, edited by Frances Mayes.
Orlando, Fla.: Harcourt Brace Jovanovich, 1987.

Keener Sounds: Selected Poems from the Georgia Review,
edited by Stanley Lindberg and Stephen Corey.
Athens: University of Georgia Press, 1987.

Poetry: The Seventy-Fifth Anniversary Issue. Chicago:
The Modern Poetry Association, 1987.

*The Made Thing: An Anthology of Contemporary
Southern Poetry,* edited by Leon Stokesbury.
Fayetteville: University of Arkansas Press, 1986,
1999 (second edition).

New American Poets of the Eighties, edited by Jack
Myers and Roger Weingarten. Green Harbor,
Mass.: Wampeter Press, 1985.

Pushcart Prize Ten: Best of the Small Presses, edited by
Bill Henderson. Wainscott, N.Y.: Avon, 1985.

The Morrow Anthology of Younger American Poets,

edited by David Smith and David Bottoms. New York: Morrow, 1984.

Pushcart Prize Nine: Best of the Small Presses, edited by Bill Henderson. Wainscott, N.Y.: Avon, 1984.

SOUND RECORDINGS

"As the Living Are to the Dead" and "Silva." Read by the author. *Cortland Review* (www.cortlandreview.com), no. 7, (May 1996).

VIDEO RECORDINGS

"Poetry Heaven" (films for the humanities and sciences, with teacher's guide). Part 1. Geraldine R. Dodge Poetry Festival, 1996. (Poetry Heaven Teacher's Guide, P.O. Box 245, Little Falls, NJ 07424-0245; 800-257-5126 for videos.)

"Pattiann Rogers Reading in Los Angeles, May 4, 1993," Lannan Literary Videos, 1993 (Small Press Distribution, Inc.; 1-800-869-7553.)

INTERVIEWS

Bryan, Sharon. "Interview: Pattiann Rogers." *River City Review* (Spring 1990): 88–112.

Elliott, David. "Praise Is a Generative Act: A Conversation with Pattiann Rogers." *Tampa Review* (Spring 1999): 19–32.

McCann, Richard. "An Interview with Pattiann Rogers." *Iowa Review* 17 (Spring/Summer 1987): 25–42.

Seale, Jan Epton. "Interview with Pattiann Rogers."
    Concho River Review 5, No. 1, (Spring, 1991): 59–64.
Seyburn, Patty. "Interview with Pattiann Rogers."
    Gulf Coast (Spring 1997): 37–41.
Walker, Casey. "An Interview with Pattiann Rogers."
    Wild Duck Review 3, no. 2 (April 1997): 7–11.
Whitehouse, Sheila Austin. "An Interview with
    Pattiann Rogers." *South Carolina Review* 25, no. 1
    (Fall 1992): 16–18.

BIOGRAPHICAL/CRITICAL STUDIES AND
    REVIEWS

Allen, Dick. "Poetry I: Charles Tomlinson, Pattiann
    Rogers, Geoffrey Hill, and Others." *Hudson Review*
    40 (Autumn 1987).
Bizzaro, Patrick. "Poetry and Audience: A Look at
    Ten Books." *Raccoon* 28 (May 1988).
Brown, Laurie. Review of *The Expectations of Light.*
    Liberty Journal (January 1982).
Brown-Davidson, Terri. Review of *Firekeeper. Prairie
    Schooner* (Fall 1996).
Budin, Sue E. Review of *Firekeeper. Kliatt* (January
    1995).
Carlisle, Susan. Review of *Firekeeper. Harvard Review*
    (May 1995).
Christopherson, Bill. Review of *Eating Bread and
    Honey. Poetry* (September 1998).
Collins, Floyd. "Motives for Metaphor." *Gettysburg
    Review* (Spring 1995).
———. "Variations on the Journey Motif." *Gettysburg
    Review* (Spring 1991).

Disch, Thomas M. Review of *Firekeeper*. *Hudson Review* (Summer 1995).

Eckman, Fred. Review of *Firekeeper*. *Star Tribune* (October 23, 1994).

Edwards, Wayne. Review of *Firekeeper*. *Small Press Review* (April 1995).

Ellis, Steven. Review of *Firekeeper*. *Library Journal* (August 1994).

Englebrecht, Marsha. "Pattiann Rogers." *Dictionary of Literary Biography*. Vol. 105. Detroit: Gale Research, 1991.

Fulton, Alice. "Main Things." *Poetry* (January 1988): 360–77.

Goding, Cecile. "Unpretty Sentences, Beautiful Structure." *Illinois Writers Review* (Spring 1992).

Grosholz, Emily. "Reviews." *Hudson Review* (June 1990).

Guereschi, Edward. "Bridesmaids and Veterans." *American Book Review* (November/December 1990).

Gunderson, Elizabeth. Review of *Firekeeper*. *Booklist* (September 1, 1994).

Gwynn, R. S. "Second Gear: Review of Leon Stokesbury, Edward Hirsch, Pattiann Rogers, and Timothy Steele." *New England Review/Breadloaf Quarterly* (Autumn 1986).

Hoagland, Tony. "*The Expectations of Light*, by Pattiann Rogers." *Telescope* (Winter 1983).

Hopes, David. "Reviews and So Forth." *Hiram Poetry Review* (Spring/Summer 1983).

Kitchen, Judith. "Fourteen Ways of Looking at Selecteds." *Georgia Review* (Summer 1995).

Martz, Louis L. "Ammons, Warren, and the Tribe of Walt." *Yale Review* 72 (Autumn 1982).

Mazur, Gail. "Brief Reviews." Review of *Splitting and Binding. Poetry* (July 1990).

McClatchy, J. D. "Short Reviews." *Poetry* (December 1983).

Merrill, Christopher. Review of *Firekeeper. Orion* (Fall 1994).

———. "Voyages into the Immediate: Recent Nature Writings." *New England Review/Breadloaf Quarterly* 10 (Spring 1988): 368–78.

Porterfield, Kay Marie. "Giving Voice to Vision." *Bloomsbury Review* (June 1991).

Ray, Janisse. Review of *Eating Bread and Honey. Orion* (Summer 1998).

Review of *Firekeeper. Publishers Weekly* (August 29, 1994).

Review of *Splitting and Binding. Publishers Weekly* (August 4, 1989).

Sampson, Dennis. Review of *Legendary Performance. Hudson Review* (Summer 1988).

Stitt, Peter. "Aestheticians and the Pit of the Self." *Poetry* (June 1988).

———. "The Objective Mode in Contemporary Lyric Poetry." *Georgia Review* 36 (Summer 1982).

Ullman, Leslie. Review of *Firekeeper. Poetry* (December 1996).

Acknowledgments for
"The Dream of the Marsh Wren"
by Pattiann Rogers

Grateful thanks to the editors of the journals in which the following previously uncollected work first appeared:

"Paganini, and Rumor as Genesis," *Gettysburg Review* 10, no. 4 (Winter 1997): 566–67.

"Before the Beginning: Maybe God and a Silk-Flower Concubine Perhaps," *Hudson Review* 50, no. 1 (Spring 1997): 97–98.

"Places within Place," *Manoa* 9, no. 1 (1997): 115–16.

"A Self-Analysis of Dust," *Palmetto Review,* no. 4 (1986): 38–39.

"Nude Standing Alone in the Forest: A Study of Place," *Poetry* 143, no. 1 (October 1983): 5–6.

"The Dream of the Marsh Wren: Reciprocal Creation" and "The Gift of Reception," *Poetry Northwest* 22, no. 3 (Autumn 1981): 5–6.

"This Nature," *Portland* (forthcoming).

"Surprised by the Sacred," *U.S. Catholic* 63, no. 3
(March 1998): 25–27.

WORKS CITED

p. 35   Roger Weingarten, "Incidental Music:
             The Grotesque, The Romantic, and The
             Retrenched," *Poetry East,* ed. Richard Jones
             and Kate Daniels, nos. 20–21 (1986):
             177–78.

p. 59   Robert Louis Stevenson, "Happy Thought,"
             in Collected Poems, 2d ed., ed. Janet Adam
             Smith (New York: The Viking Press, 1971),
             375.

pp. 64–65 "View of Distant, Faint Galaxies Reveals
             Young Galaxy Building Blocks," from text
             accompanying images captured by the
             Hubble Space Telescope, photo no. STScI-
             PRC96-29a (September 4, 1996). Credit by
             Rogier Windhorst and Sam Pascarelle
             (Arizona State University) and NASA.
             Found on the internet: http://oposite.
             stsci.edu/pubinfo/PR/96/29/A.html.

pp. 85–86   D. H. Lawrence, "Snake," in *The Complete Poems of D. H. Lawrence,* ed. V. de Sola Pinto and F. W. Roberts (New York: Penguin, 1964), 349–50. Copyright © 1964, 1971 by Angelo Ravagli and C. M. Wackley, executors of the estate of Frieda Lawrence Ravagli. Used by permission of Viking Penguin, a division of Penguin Putnam, Inc.

p. 86   Walt Whitman, "Song of Myself," in *Walt Whitman: Complete Poetry and Collected Prose* (New York: The Library of America, 1982), 190.

p. 88   Issa, "The Great Buddha at Nara," in *An Introduction to Haiku: An Anthology of Poems and Poets from Bashō to Shiki,* ed. and trans. Harold G. Henderson (Garden City, N.Y.: Doubleday Anchor Books, 1958), 139. Copyright © 1958 by Harold G. Henderson. Used by permission of Doubleday, a division of Random House, Inc.

p. 88   Issa, "Heaven's River," in *An Introduction to Haiku,* 148. Copyright © 1958 by Harold G. Henderson. Used by permission of Doubleday, a division of Random House, Inc.

p. 89   Walt Whitman, "Song of Myself," 217.

pp. 89–90   Jacob Bronowski, *The Ascent of Man* (Boston: Little, Brown and Co., 1973), 417, 421.

p. 90   Walt Whitman, "I Sing the Body Electric," in *Walt Whitman: Complete Poetry and Collected Prose* (New York: The Library of America, 1982), 122.

p. 92   Walt Whitman, "Song of Myself," 244.

p. 92   Barry Lopez, *Arctic Dreams: Imagination and Desire in a Northern Landscape* (New York: Charles Scribner's Sons, 1986), 250.

p. 92   John Berryman, "Eleven Addresses to the Lord," in *John Berryman: Collected Poems 1937–1971,* ed. Charles Thornbury (New York: Farrar, Straus, Giroux, 1989), 215. Copyright © 1989 by Kate Donahue Berryman. Reprinted by permission of Farrar, Straus & Giroux, Inc.

p. 92   Rainer Maria Rilke, "Buddha in Glory," in *The Selected Poetry of Rainer Maria Rilke,* ed. and trans. Stephen Mitchell (New York: Random House, 1982), 69. Copyright © 1982 by Stephen Mitchell. Reprinted by permission of Random House, Inc.

p. 104   Pattiann Rogers, "What Among Heavens and Suns," *Orion Society Notebook* (Autumn/Winter 1996).

p. 105 Richard McCann, "An Interview with Pattiann Rogers," *Iowa Review* 17, no. 2 (Spring/Summer 1987): 25.

p. 106 Richard McCann, "An Interview with Pattiann Rogers," 29.

p. 107 Pattiann Rogers, letter to Scott Slovic, (April 1, 1998).

p. 108 Pattiann Rogers, letter to Scott Slovic, (April 1, 1998).

p. 109 Pattiann Rogers, letter to Scott Slovic, (April 1, 1998).

p. 109 Pattiann Rogers, letter to Scott Slovic, (April 1, 1998).

p. 110 Casey Walker, "An Interview with Pattiann Rogers," *Wild Duck Review* 3, no. 2 (April 1997): 10.

p. 111 Peter Stitt, "The Objective Mode in Contemporary Lyric Poetry," *Georgia Review* 36, no. 2 (Summer 1982): 442.

p. 111 Werner Heisenberg, quoted in McCann, "An Interview with Pattiann Rogers," 27.

pp. 112–13 Marsha Engelbrecht, "Pattiann Rogers," in Dictionary of Literary Biography, ed. R. S. Gwynn (Detroit: Gale Research, 1991), 214.

pp. 113–14 Leslie Ullman, review of *Firekeeper, Poetry* (December 1996): 161.

p. 114   Pattiann Rogers, "Animals and People: 'The
            Human Heart in Conflict with Itself,'" in
            Eating Bread and Honey (Minneapolis:
            Milkweed Editions, 1997), 36.

p. 115   Rogers, "The Fallacy of Thinking Flesh Is
            Flesh," in *Eating Bread and Honey,* 10.

p. 115   Ullman, review of *Firekeeper,* 162.

SCOTT SLOVIC, founding president of the Association for the Study of Literature and Environment (ASLE), currently serves as editor of the journal *ISLE: Interdisciplinary Studies in Literature and Environment.* He is the author of *Seeking Awareness in American Nature Writing: Henry Thoreau, Annie Dillard, Edward Abbey, Wendell Berry, Barry Lopez* (University of Utah Press, 1992); his coedited books include *Being in the World: An Environmental Reader for Writers* (Macmillan, 1993), *Reading the Earth: New Directions in the Study of Literature and the Environment* (University of Idaho Press, 1998), and *Literature and the Environment: A Reader on Nature and Culture* (Addison Wesley Longman, 1999). Currently he is an associate professor of English and the director of the Center for Environmental Arts and Humanities at the University of Nevada, Reno.

More Books from Milkweed Editions

To order books or for more information,
contact Milkweed at (800) 520-6455
or visit our website (www.milkweed.org).

The Credo Series

Brown Dog of the Yaak:
Rick Bass

Winter Creek
John Daniel

Writing the Sacred into the Real
Alison Hawthorne Deming

The Frog Run
John Elder

Taking Care
William Kittredge

An American Child Supreme
John Nichols

Walking the High Ridge
Robert Michael Pyle

The Dream of the Marsh Wren
Pattiann Rogers

The Country of Language
Scott Russell Sanders

Shaped by Wind and Water
Ann Haymond Zwinger

Typeset in Stone Serif
by Stanton Publication Services, Inc.
Printed on acid-free,
recycled 55# Frasier Miami Book Natural paper
by Friesen Corporation.